TRADE ISSUES, POLICIES AND LAWS

U.S. TRADE PREFERENCES FOR DEVELOPING COUNTRIES

TRADE ISSUES, POLICIES AND LAWS

Additional books in this series can be found on Nova's website under the Series tab.

Additional E-books in this series can be found on Nova's website under the E-books tab.

ECONOMIC ISSUES, PROBLEMS AND PERSPECTIVES

Additional books in this series can be found on Nova's website under the Series tab.

Additional E-books in this series can be found on Nova's website under the E-books tab.

TRADE ISSUES, POLICIES AND LAWS

U.S. TRADE PREFERENCES FOR DEVELOPING COUNTRIES

JONATHAN R. FERREIRA
EDITOR

Nova Science Publishers, Inc.
New York

For permission to use material from this book please contact us:
Telephone 631-231-7269; Fax 631-231-8175
Web Site: http://www.novapublishers.com

Library of Congress Cataloging-in-Publication Data

U.S. trade preferences for developing countries / editors, Jonathan R. Ferreira.
p. cm.
"CRS Report for Congress prepared for members and committees of Congress."
Includes bibliographical references and index.
ISBN 978-1-61324-378-7 (hardcover)
1. Tariff preferences--Law and legislation--United States. 2. Tariff preferences--Developing countries. 3. United States--Foreign economic relations--Developing countries. 4. Developing countries--Foreign economic relations--United States. I. Ferreira, Jonathan R. II. Library of Congress. Congressional Research Service. III. Title: United States trade preferences for developing countries.
KF6708.P7U17 2011
343.73'087--dc22

2011013417

Published by Nova Science Publishers, Inc. † New York

CONTENTS

PREFACE

Congress has created multiple trade preference programs designed to foster economic growth, reform and development in less developed countries. These programs give temporary, non-reciprocal, duty-free U.S. market access to select exports of eligible countries. Congress conducts regular oversight of these programs, repeatedly revising and extending them. This book discusses the major U.S. trade preference programs, their possible economic effects, stakeholder interests and legislative options.

Chapter 1- Since 1974, Congress has created multiple trade preference programs designed to foster economic growth, reform, and development in less developed countries. These programs give temporary, non-reciprocal, duty-free U.S. market access to select exports of eligible countries. Congress conducts regular oversight of these programs, repeatedly revising and extending them.

Congress established five trade preference programs. The Generalized System of Preferences (GSP) applies to developing countries as a whole. In addition, there are four regional programs established in the Andean Trade Preference Act (APTA), the Caribbean Basin Economic Recovery Act (CBERA); the Caribbean Trade Partnership Act (CBTPA), the African Growth and Opportunity Act (AGOA), and the Haitian Opportunity through Partnership Encouragement (HOPE) Act. Both the GSP and the ATPA are scheduled to expire on December 31, 2010.

Chapter 2- Article I:1 of the General Agreement on Tariffs and Trade 1994 (GATT 1994) requires World Trade Organization (WTO) Members to grant most-favored-nation (MFN) treatment "immediately and unconditionally" to the like products of other Members with respect to tariffs and other trade-related measures. Programs such as the Generalized System of Preferences (GSP), under which developed countries grant preferential tariff rates to developing country goods, are facially inconsistent with this obligation because they accord goods of some countries more favorable tariff treatment than that accorded to like goods of other WTO Members. Because such programs have been viewed as trade-expanding, however, parties to the GATT provided a legal basis for one-way tariff preferences in a 1979 decision known as the Enabling Clause. The Enabling Clause was formally incorporated into the GATT 1994 upon the entry into force of the GATT Uruguay Round agreements on January 1, 1995. In 2004, the WTO Appellate Body ruled that the Clause allows developed countries to offer differing treatment to developing countries in a GSP program, but only if identical treatment is available to all similarly situated beneficiaries.

Chapter 3- The U.S. Generalized System of Preferences (GSP) program provides non-reciprocal, duty-free tariff treatment to certain products imported from designated beneficiary developing countries (BDCs). The United States, the European Union, and other developed countries have implemented similar programs since the 1970s in order to promote economic growth in developing countries by stimulating their exports. The U.S. program was first authorized in Title V of the Trade Act of 1974, and was most recently extended until December 31, 2010, in P.L. 111-124 for all GSP beneficiary countries not covered by the African Growth and Opportunity Act (AGOA). Since GSP will expire at the end of 2010, this and other trade preference programs may continue to be a the focus of congressional attention in the 112th Congress.

Chapter 4- The Generalized System of Preferences (GSP) provides duty-free tariff treatment for certain products from designated developing countries. Agricultural imports under the GSP totaled $2.2 billion in 2009, about 11% of all U.S. GSP imports. Leading agricultural imports include processed foods and food processing inputs, sugar and sugar confectionery, cocoa, processed and fresh fruits and vegetables, beverages and drinking waters, olive oil, processed meats, and miscellaneous food preparations and inputs for further processing. The majority of these imports are from Thailand, Brazil, Argentina, India, and the Philippines. Some in Congress have continued to call for changes to the program that could limit GSP benefits to certain countries, among other changes. Opinion within the U.S. agriculture industry is mixed, reflecting both support for and opposition to the current program. Congress made changes to the program in 2006, tightening its requirements on imports under certain circumstances.

Chapter 5- In May 2008, Vietnam formally requested to be added to the U.S. Generalized System of Preferences (GSP) program as a "developing country." On June 20, 2008, the office of the U.S. Trade Representative (USTR) announced that it was initiating a formal review of Vietnam's eligibility for GSP benefits and would accept public comments on the application until August 4, 2008. Vietnam has already been accepted into several other developed-country GSP programs around the world, including Canada, the European Union (EU), and Japan.

In: U.S. Trade Preferences…
Editor: Jonathan R. Ferreira

ISBN: 978-1-61324-378-7

Chapter 1

TRADE PREFERENCES: ECONOMIC ISSUES AND POLICY OPTIONS*

Vivian C. Jones, J. F. Hornbeck and M. Angeles Villarreal

SUMMARY

Since 1974, Congress has created multiple trade preference programs designed to foster economic growth, reform, and development in less developed countries. These programs give temporary, non-reciprocal, duty-free U.S. market access to select exports of eligible countries. Congress conducts regular oversight of these programs, repeatedly revising and extending them.

Congress established five trade preference programs. The Generalized System of Preferences (GSP) applies to developing countries as a whole. In addition, there are four regional programs established in the Andean Trade Preference Act (APTA), the Caribbean Basin Economic Recovery Act (CBERA); the Caribbean Trade Partnership Act (CBTPA), the African Growth and Opportunity Act (AGOA), and the Haitian Opportunity through Partnership Encouragement (HOPE) Act.

* This is an edited, reformatted and augmented version of a Congressional Research Services publication, CRS Report for Congress R41429, from www.crs.gov, dated September 24, 2010.

Both the GSP and the ATPA are scheduled to expire on December 31, 2010.

Unlike free trade agreements, trade preferences are unilateral, so developing countries do not have to provide reciprocal trade benefits to the United States. To qualify for tariff preferences, however, they must meet certain eligibility criteria, which vary by program. Examples include adopting internationally recognized worker rights, providing adequate protection of intellectual property rights, and operating an open market economy under established multilateral trade rules. In the 111th Congress, the House Ways and Means and Senate Finance Committees have held hearings on the operation and impact of these programs. In the first session, Congress legislatively extended the GSP and ATPA for a one-year, ending December 31, 2010 (P.L. 111- 124). In the second session, it has extended provisions in the CBPTA and HOPE Act through September 30, 2020 in the Haiti Economic Lift Program Act of 2010 (P.L. 111-171). Other bills introduced include H.R. 1837 and S. 1665, which would extend ATPA to additional countries; and S. 1141 and S. 4101, which would expand product coverage for certain least-developed countries.

Trade preferences are permitted by the World Trade Organization (WTO) under the General Agreement on Tariffs and Trade (GATT) "enabling clause," which allows members to provide more favorable treatment to developing countries. Other developed countries such as Canada, Japan, the European Union (EU), and Australia provide similar preferences. In the WTO Doha Development Agenda (DDA) round of multilateral trade negotiations, both developed and developing WTO members agreed to provide duty-free, quota-free (DFQF) preferential access to least-developed countries, subject to adoption of the agreement.

Evaluations of the benefits of trade preferences have been mixed. Many developing countries have used tariff preferences to enhance their competitiveness in certain industries, particularly apparel. In other countries, preferences are used to export major commodities such as petroleum products, which may be less supportive of long-term economic diversification and development. Meeting the needs of the least developing countries is a core policy issue that continues to drive the debate over the design of preference programs. Consumers and some U.S. industries and workers benefit from the additional trade, others compete directly with it, so perspectives on trade preferences vary despite their overall costs apparently being small.

This report discusses the major U.S. trade preference programs, their possible economic effects, stakeholder interests, and legislative options.

INTRODUCTION

Since 1974, Congress has created multiple trade preference programs designed to foster economic growth and development in less developed countries. These programs give temporary, non-reciprocal, duty-free U.S. market access to select exports of eligible countries. Congress conducts regular oversight of these programs, often revising and extending them.

BACKGROUND

The multilateral trading system that has evolved since the end of World War II is centered on the guiding tenet of nondiscrimination. It is embodied in the most favored nation (MFN) principle of the General Agreement on Tariffs and Trade (GATT) and its successor, the World Trade Organization (WTO).[1] The economic rationale for this foundational idea rests on avoiding the type of protectionist policies prominent during the inter-war period that exacerbated the Great Depression. As fundamental as MFN treatment is to the conduct of modern trade, the GATT/WTO also allows for certain exceptions, one being special and differential treatment (SDT) for developing countries.

Special trade treatment permits, among other policies, preferential programs that reduce tariffs on certain goods from eligible developing countries. Lower tariffs support an export development strategy that is based on increasing trade and diversifying it away from traditional commodity exports into more value-added goods in industry and manufacturing. Because commodity prices have declined over the long run and experienced periods of extreme volatility over shorter periods of time, countries dependent on them often find their trade position weakened over time.[2] Exports are also key to development of industry in countries with small domestic markets. By diversifying trade to other sectors and industries it is hoped that developing economies will attract more investment, create more jobs, become more stable, and grow faster.[3]

Many developed countries have unilateral trade preference programs; Congress has legislatively established five in the United States. The first was the Generalized System of Preferences (GSP), established in the Trade Act of 1974. It applies to developing countries as a whole. In addition, there are four regional programs that followed, created in the Andean Trade Preference Act (APTA), the Caribbean Basin Economic Recovery Act (CBERA); the

Caribbean Basin Trade Partnership Act (CBTPA), the African Growth and Opportunity Act (AGOA), and the Haitian Opportunity through Partnership Encouragement (HOPE) Act (discussed in detail below). The regional programs were built on the GSP concept, but are more targeted and tend to offer more generous and flexible access to the U.S. market.

Trade preferences provide duty-free U.S. market access to select exports of eligible developing countries. All U.S. preference programs are unilateral, meaning that they do not require reciprocal trade concessions. Congress conducts oversight of these programs, revising and extending them periodically.[4] In order to qualify to receive benefits, beneficiary developing countries must meet eligibility criteria, which vary by program. Some examples include ensuring that prospective countries make strides toward enhancing the rule of law, adopting internationally recognized worker rights, supporting counternarcotics policies, and providing open markets for U.S. exports. Preference programs, as such, are regarded by many as integral elements of U.S. trade, development, and foreign policy.

During the 111th Congress, both the House Ways and Means and Senate Finance Committees have held hearings to evaluate preference programs and possible means to improve their effectiveness. Congress passed legislation in the first session that extends the GSP and ATPA for one year through December 31, 2010 (P.L. 111-124). In the second session, Congress has extended the CBPTA through September 30, 2020, and granted additional preferences to Haiti in the Haiti Economic Lift Program Act of 2010 (P.L. 111-171). Other bills introduced include H.R. 1837 and S. 1665, which would expand the ATPA to additional countries; and S. 1141 and S. 4101, which would expand product coverage for certain least-developed countries, but Congress has not acted on these legislative initiatives.

Supporters of trade preferences include beneficiary developing country governments who have established industries and jobs partially as a result of preference programs, U.S. importers, including retailers and U.S. consuming industries, and U.S. producers working in joint production with assembly plants in developing countries. These groups tend to favor longer-term renewal of preferences to ensure more predictability, which is one important factor in investment and sourcing decisions. Stakeholders opposed to preference programs include U.S. manufacturers of competing import-sensitive products and some labor groups representing workers negatively affected by them, although the strict labor requirements of preference programs can attract support from labor groups. Generally, preference programs receive broad support in Congress, but some lawmakers have reservations about their design and operation.

Generalized System of Preferences (GSP)

Authorized by Congress in 1974, the GSP is the oldest and largest trade preference program, currently providing trade benefits to 131 countries. It was last extended through December 31, 2010, by P.L. 111-124. The GSP statute (Title V of the Trade Act of 1974, P.L. 93-618, as amended) authorizes the President to grant duty-free status to selected imports from two categories of countries: beneficiary developing countries (BDCs) and least-developed country beneficiaries (LDBDCs),[5] the latter designating additional special treatment for the poorest developing countries.[6] The President may designate eligible countries, subject to various mandatory and discretionary conditions as set out in the statute.[7] In general, these include: providing equitable and reasonable market access; taking actions to adopt internationally recognized worker rights; supporting private ownership and repatriation of capital; not engaging in practices that would harm U.S. economic interests; and supporting certain U.S. anti-terrorism policies.[8] The GSP program is implemented by the Trade Policy Staff Committee (TPSC), an interagency group chaired by the Office of the U.S. Trade Representative (USTR).

In order to qualify for GSP eligibility, products must be imported directly from a BDC, where at least 35% of the value of materials and/or processing must be completed.[9] The President is authorized to designate products as eligible for GSP status, but many agricultural, textile, apparel, and other "import sensitive" products are excluded.[10] In addition, a country (LDC beneficiaries excluded) may lose eligibility for a particular product due to statutory competitive need limitations (CNLs). An automatic CNL is triggered if imports of a product from a BDC: (1) exceed a specified threshold value ($140 million in 2010); or (2) account for 50% or more of total U.S. imports of the product. After the threshold is reached, CNLs go into effect on July 1 of the next calendar year and may be waived under certain conditions.[11]

Countries are also mandatorily "graduated" from the GSP program if the President determines that they have become a "high income" country.[12] Benefits may also be limited or withdrawn if the President determines that a beneficiary is sufficiently competitive based an assessment of its level of economic development, per capita income, or living standards.[13]

Regional Programs

The Caribbean

In 1983, Congress created the first regionally-targeted preference program with strong bipartisan passage of the Caribbean Basin Economic Recovery Act (CBERA).[14] The Act provided limited duty-free entry of select Caribbean exports as a core element of the U.S. foreign economic policy response to deteriorating economic and political conditions in the region in the 1980s. Although considered an important new program at the time, its effects were limited by the exclusion of key exports, especially apparel. Apparel were (and are) major products of the region, but were designated "import sensitive" in the United States. CBERA was made permanent with a few modest additions of eligible products in the Caribbean Basin Economic Expansion Act of 1990 (CBI II).[15]

Additional preferences were extended to the Caribbean region in the Caribbean Basin Trade Partnership Act (CBTPA) in May 2000.[16] In the CBTPA, Congress effectively extended benefits to eligible Caribbean countries through fiscal year 2008 equivalent to those given to Mexico under the North American Free Trade Agreement (NAFTA). The CBPTA also enhanced product coverage to include certain apparel goods—provided that the fabrics were sourced in the United States or the Caribbean and made from U.S. yarn. Congress recently extended CBTPA through September 30, 2020 in the Haiti Economic Lift Program (HELP) Act of 2010.[17]

Implementation of the Dominican Republic-Central America-United States Free Trade Agreement (CAFTA-DR) on March 1, 2006 shifted treatment of imports from the largest Caribbean apparel producing countries from a unilateral preference program to the more liberal benefits afforded under the new, reciprocal free trade agreement (FTA).[18] Haiti was the only major apparel-producing country in the region that was not included in CAFTA-DR.[19] Because Haiti's economic fortunes continued to deteriorate, Congress provided uniquely generous and flexible unilateral preferences to Haiti's apparel sector by amending CBERA to include the Haitian Hemispheric Opportunity through Partnership Encouragement Act of 2006 (HOPE I).[20] These preferences were further enhanced and extended by the HOPE II Act of 2008,[21] and again by the HELP Act.

The HOPE Act, as amended, differs from other U.S. preference programs because it allows duty-free treatment for Haitian apparel exports made from limited amounts of lower-cost third-country fabrics and other inputs from countries outside the region or not part of a trade agreement with the United

State (e.g., many Asian producers). The eligibility criteria are based on GSP provisions, with an additional requirement mandating detailed United Nations monitoring of Haitian firms to ensure that they conform to internationally recognized worker rights.[22]

Andean Trade Preference Act (ATPA)

The United States originally extended special duty treatment to imports from Colombia, Ecuador, Peru, and Bolivia in the Andean Trade Preference Act (ATPA), initially enacted on December 4, 1991, and most recently extended through December 31, 2010.[23] It lapsed on December 4, 2001, but was subsequently renewed and amended on August 6, 2002 in the Andean Trade Promotion and Drug Eradication Act (ATPDEA).[24] ATPDEA renewed ATPA trade preferences and also expanded the preferences to include additional products previously excluded under ATPA, including certain petroleum and petroleum products, textiles and apparel, footwear, and tuna in flexible containers, among others.

The purpose of ATPA is to provide preferential duty treatment to U.S. imports from beneficiary countries to promote economic growth, provide "legitimate" business opportunities, and expand job creation as alternatives to illegal crop production and drug trafficking.[25] The ATPA is one part of a broader U.S. initiative to address the drug trade problem in the Andean region. Other efforts include drug crop eradication and additional counter-narcotics activities.

In December 2008, then-President George W. Bush determined that Bolivia failed to meet ATPA beneficiary criteria and suspended Bolivia's status as a beneficiary country for failure to cooperate in counternarcotics efforts. On June 30, 2009, President Barack Obama extended this determination. Reinstatement of Bolivia as an ATPA beneficiary country will require congressional approval.

African Growth and Opportunity Act (AGOA)

The African Growth and Opportunity Act (AGOA)[26] originated in 2000 as part of an increasing U.S. effort to promote the development of, and deeper economic integration with, sub-Saharan Africa. The preference program was last amended and renewed through September 30, 2015.[27] GSP benefits were also extended to AGOA-eligible countries until that time, irrespective of any other congressional determinations on GSP extension.[28]

AGOA provides eligible sub-Saharan African countries more generous duty-free access than afforded under GSP, including special access for certain textile and apparel products that are designated "import sensitive" in the GSP statute.[29] AGOA also provides U.S. technical assistance and trade capacity building to eligible governments and businesses through four regional trade hubs in Gaborone, Botswana; Nairobi, Kenya; Accra, Ghana; and Dakar, Senegal.[30]

Currently, 38 countries are eligible to receive AGOA benefits. AGOA-eligible countries must demonstrate, among other things, that they: (1) are making continual progress toward establishing a market-based economy; (2) do not engage in activities that undermine U.S. national security and foreign policy interests; and (3) do not engage in gross violations of internationally recognized human rights or provide support for international terrorism.[31]

PREFERENCE PROGRAMS AND THE WTO

The GATT and WTO agreements are based on the fundamental principle that unconditional mostfavored-nation (non-discriminatory) status must be offered to the products of other Members with respect to tariffs and other trade-related measures.[32] Programs offering preferential treatment, such as the GSP, are inconsistent with this principle. Because these programs were designed to help less developed countries through trade expansion, parties to the GATT provided a legal basis for one-way tariff preferences in the 1979 "Enabling Clause," which stated that "contracting parties may accord differential and more favorable treatment to developing countries, without according such treatment to other contracting parties" under certain conditions.[33] The Enabling Clause was formally incorporated into the GATT 1994 when the Uruguay Round Agreements— the same agreements that established the WTO—entered into force on January 1, 1995.

Other developed countries offer special trade preferences for developing countries including Canada, the European Union, Japan, and Australia.[34] Some developing nations, such as India and Brazil, also provide tariff concessions to least developed countries (LDCs).[35] Generally, each preference-granting country extends to eligible developing countries (as determined by each benefactor) an exemption from duties (in the form of duty-free access or reduced tariffs) on designated "non-sensitive" manufactured products and agricultural goods. Product coverage and the type of preferential treatment offered vary widely.[36] Although most preference schemes (including all U.S. programs) admit eligible products duty-free, some countries provide tariff reductions, rather than complete exemption, from duties. The Australian system, for example, is based on a five percentage point margin of preference, meaning that when the Australian General Tariff (GT) is 5% or higher on a given product, the amount of the tariff is reduced by 5 percentage points for products of beneficiary countries. When the GT rate is 5% or less, the preferential rate is zero.[37]

Other developed countries also offer regional preferences, or preferences that "reward" developing countries that comply with additional eligibility criteria such as anti-corruption measures, environmental sustainability goals, or core worker rights provisions. For example, the European Union offers additional duty-free access to its market to LDC beneficiaries under the "Everything But Arms" preference,[38] as well as an incentive-based program (known as GSP+) that provides enhanced benefits for "vulnerable countries" (in terms of size or limited diversification in its exports). GSP+ beneficiaries must have ratified and effectively implemented 27 specified international conventions in the fields of human rights, core labor standards, sustainable development, and good governance.[39]

Also in the WTO, as a part of the Doha Round of multilateral trade negotiations, developed country members and "developing country members declaring themselves in a position to do so" agreed to provide "duty-free and quota-free" (DFQF) market access for all products originating from all least-developed countries "in a manner that ensures stability, security, and predictability."[40] Members "facing difficulties" would be permitted to exempt 3% of all tariff lines, provided that steps are taken to build the list of covered products until total DFQF is reached.[41] Since the DDA is a "single undertaking" (which means that nothing is finally agreed until everything is agreed), the DFQF agreement reached in 2005, will not be implemented until the negotiating round is concluded.[42]

Stakeholder Perspectives

Like all public policies, the costs and benefits do not fall uniformly to all affected parties. This is reflected in various stakeholder responses to trade preferences. Supporters include beneficiary developing country governments, producers, workers, and exporters. Many of these countries receive foreign investment based on U.S. trade preferences, resulting in increased employment in certain industries.[43] For these countries, jobs and related income created by U.S. trade preference programs have become an important element for economic growth and development. Many beneficiary stakeholders express concern that if preferences are not renewed, other low-cost countries such as China would benefit at their expense.[44]

U.S. manufacturers who import intermediate products through the various trade preference programs in downstream products also support trade preferences. Some U.S. producers, especially in the U.S. textile and apparel industries, have made use of preferences to remain competitive through cooperative relationships with certain beneficiaries, especially the Caribbean and Latin American countries.[45] Businesses that benefit from preference programs favor longer-term renewal of trade preferences because they provide predictability when signing import contracts and making investment decisions.[46]

Trade preferences reflect both economic development and foreign policy goals. In addition to the economic benefits, eligibility criteria create incentives for beneficiary countries to support U.S. objectives such as adopting and enforcing internationally recognized worker rights, reducing barriers to investment, and enforcing intellectual property rights.[47] In addition, U.S. regional preferences created with particular goals in mind—such as eradication of drug production in the case of the Andean trade preference program—create incentives to fulfill additional U.S. policy goals.[48] Organized labor, for example, tends to support trade preferences because worker rights provisions have led to improvements in labor rights in some regions. Labor officials have cited the GSP process, specifically annual country practice reviews, as helpful in addressing enforcement and rule-of-law issues relating to compliance.[49] Labor support, however, is also tempered by the fact that certain workers will be negatively affected by increased imports of products with which they compete.

Stakeholders opposed to preferences programs mostly include U.S. manufacturers of competing import-sensitive products. In particular, some in the U.S. textile and apparel industry are opposed to unfettered extension of textile and apparel preferences, especially when U.S. workers are potentially adversely affected.[50]

ECONOMIC ISSUES

All trade preference programs have in common the goal to promote export-driven growth and development in less developed countries. The programs themselves, however, raise multiple economic and political issues. Preference program features are a key factor in determining their effectiveness. Among key issues is the extent to which preferences: (1) target the developing country's productive capacity; (2) have sufficiently flexible and manageable rules of origin; (3) are not overly restricted by domestic interests; and (4) are extended for a sufficiently long period of time to attract foreign investment. Because of eligibility requirements that countries must accept from the preference giver, and the fact that they can also be unilaterally cut off, there are also opportunity costs to preferences.[51]

Program Effectiveness—Use of U.S. Trade Preferences

The value trade preferences provide from a programmatic perspective rests on their ability to increase exports from developing countries, particularly away from traditional commodities. The value to the exporting countries is equal to what is called the preference margin, which may be simply defined as the difference between the MFN and preferential tariffs on exported goods.[52] If the preference margin is significant, it should contribute to export growth by reducing the import cost of goods in the United States relative to competing exports from countries without preferences.

One simple approach to examining the benefits of preference programs is to evaluate their use by observed growth in exports, although this provides for only a preliminary understanding.[53] For example, the total value of imports entering under U.S. preference programs in 2008 was $110.0 billion in 2008, and $60.5 billion in 2009 (see *Figure* **1** and *Table 1*). U.S. imports from all countries fell dramatically in 2009, including those entering under preference programs. The Great Recession was the major cause of U.S. import compression in 2009, with the decline in U.S. consumption of petroleum products being a key trend. For AGOA in particular, the dramatic decline in 2009 reflects that 93% of AGOA-eligible imports are petroleum products, the demand for which fell precipitously with the economic downturn (see Appendix *Table A-2* for data). Such a dramatic fall in exports entering under preference programs points to two fundamental concerns: the continued dependence on price-volatile commodity exports, and the possible failure of preference programs to encourage greater export diversification.

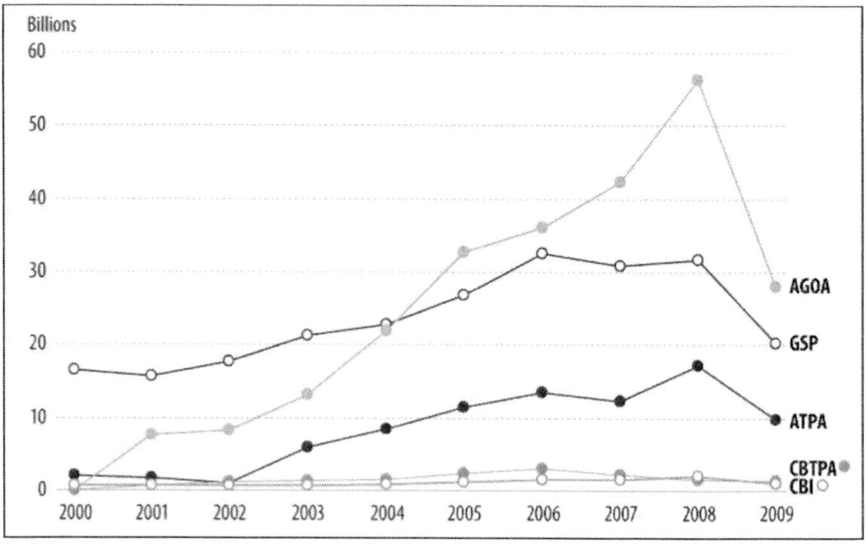

Source: United States International Trade Commission Trade Dataweb, http://www.usitc.gov.

Figure 1. Imports Entering Under Preference Programs, 2000-2009 (in billions of U.S. Dollars).

Table 1. Imports by Preference Program (in billions of U.S. Dollars)

Trade Preference Program	2000	2001	2002	2003	2004	2005	2006	2007	2008	2009
GSP	16.4	15.7	17.7	21.3	22.7	26.7	32.6	30.8	31.7	20.3
ATPA	2.0	1.7	1.0	5.8	8.4	11.5	13.5	12.3	17.2	9.7
AGOA	0	7.6	8.3	13.2	22.0	32.7	36.1	42.3	56.4	28.1
CBERA	2.6	2.7	2.9	3.0	2.9	3.4	4.0	2.8	3.0	1.1
CBTPA	0.2	5.6	7.1	7.5	7.9	8.8	6.0	2.7	1.7	1.3
Total	21.2	33.3	37.0	50.8	63.9	83.1	92.2	90.9	110.0	60.5

Source: United States International Trade Commission Trade Dataweb, http://dataweb.usitc.gov.

Figure 2 illustrates that only 5.2% of about $1.3 trillion in U.S. imports entered duty-free under preference programs in 2008.[54] About 16% of U.S. imports entered duty-free (or at reduced duties) under reciprocally negotiated free trade agreements (FTAs). In 2008, the largest percentage (79%) of U.S.

imports entered under most-favored-nation (MFN), also known as normal trade relations (NTR) rates.[55] The simple average U.S. tariff rate is 3.3%, but tariffs on certain items, including some eligible under preference programs, are much higher.[56]

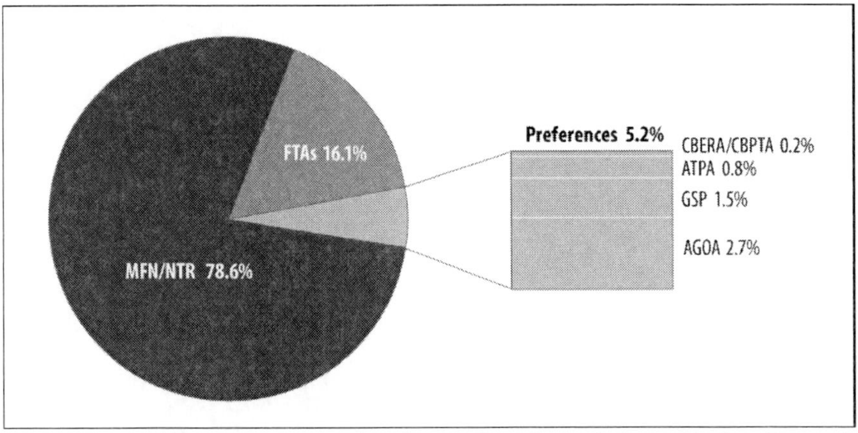

Source: United States International Trade Commission Trade Dataweb, http://dataweb.usitc.gov.

Figure 2. Preference Programs as a Percentage of All U.S. Imports, 2008.

Preference margins, by and large, tend to be small, providing relatively limited benefit to developing countries. More nuanced findings suggest, however, that certain products with high tariffs, such as apparel, provide a much greater benefit to those countries able to produce for the U.S. market. At the other end of the spectrum, the preference margin on petroleum is much smaller because tariffs tend to be small or zero in the case of many countries, and so there is much less benefit from a particular preference program. Nor does continuing to rely on petroleum exports promote economic diversification conducive for development.[57]

There are also costs associated with tariff preferences. Extensive administrative procedures and complex rules of origin often diminish their use. Also, benefits may accrue to U.S. importers rather than exporters, if they are price setters in the domestic economy. Preferences may also diminish production of competing goods in the importing country and cause some trade diversion.[58]

Figure 3 illustrates foreign direct investment (FDI) flows to beneficiary countries by preference program from 2000 to 2009, although attributing these trends to preference programs is analytically difficult. Nonetheless, between

2000 and 2008, the most dramatic increases in FDI flows occurred in GSP beneficiary countries. These countries received more than $350 billion in foreign investment in 2008. AGOA countries also experienced slow, but steady FDI growth, from $24.8 billion in 2000 to $46.5 billion in 2008. ATPA countries, likewise, experienced slow, steady increases in FDI flows. FDI flows to Latin American and Caribbean beneficiaries of CBERA and CBTPA remained relatively stable during the period. As with the record on imports, the decline in investment from 2008 to 2009 can be attributed largely to the global economic downturn.

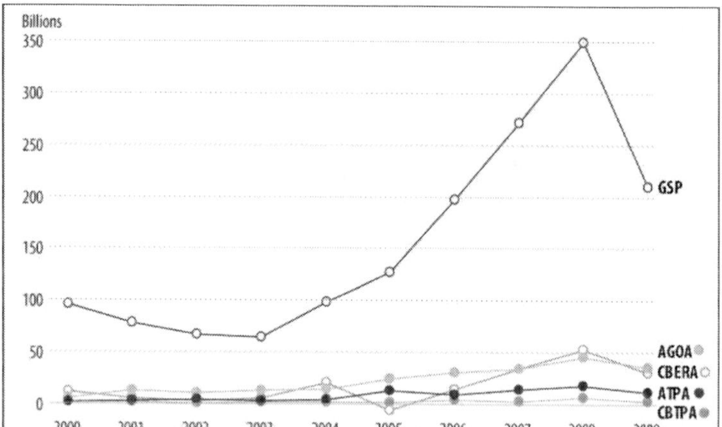

Source: United Nations Conference on Trade and Development (UNCTAD), Foreign Direct Investment Database.

Figure 3. Foreign Investment Flows to Preference Receiving Countries, 2000-2009 (in billions of U.S. dollars).

Developing Country Economic Effects

For GSP countries, total U.S. imports from all BDCs have increased 250% over a twelve-year time period, from $107.8 billion in 1996 to $378.0 billion in 2008. Over the same time period, total U.S. imports entering under the GSP program increased at a slower rate, from $11.6 billion to $31.2 billion in 2008.[59] Together, these data indicate that only about 10% of exports from eligible countries enter the United States under the GSP program, a relationship that has remained steady or declined slightly over time.[60] Thus, in the aggregate, the GSP affects a relatively small portion of developing country exports. This is due, in part, to program restrictions on key "import sensitive" exports such as textiles and apparel and agricultural goods, and is also perhaps due in part to the automatic CNLs on GSP-eligible products. Mandatory graduation of beneficiaries from the GSP may also be a factor.

The Caribbean programs have had varying economic effects depending on how they have been structured. The original CBERA program provided few incentives to the major exports of the region (i.e., apparel), and so the response was predictably limited. This remained unchanged until the CBTPA, passed in 2000, provided duty-free treatment for apparel, among other goods. Since Central America is a major source of apparel goods, it was not surprising that U.S. imports under CBTPA grew to some 30% of total imports from the region by 2003. Nonetheless, U.S. imports of apparel under CBTPA continued to shrink as a percentage of apparel imports from the world, perhaps pointing to the limits of preferential tariff treatment in the face of a highly competitive global market. With the implementation of the CAFTA-DR, apparel concessions were more favorable under the agreement and so were no longer exported under the Caribbean preferences. This trend is reflected in the decline of total imports from CBERA countries from $31.8 billion in 2005 to $19.6 billion in 2008, with goods imported under the CBTPA falling from 28% in 2005 to only 9% of total imports from the region by 2008.[61]

The Haiti HOPE I Act was used minimally in the first two years, because of its highly complicated rules of origin and a short-term extension by Congress that did not entice investor response. With the passage of HOPE II, the preferences were made more flexible and generous, targeted to both knit and woven textiles and apparel. Simpler rules of origin, particularly those that did not require use of U.S. or domestic materials, were widely used. This again points to the importance of preference program design as a critical factor for predicting their use. Congress amended and enhanced the preferences on products that were imported most frequently under the preference when passing the HELP Act of 2010.[62]

The effect of the ATPA on the economies of Bolivia, Colombia, Ecuador, and Peru has also been small but positive. A study by the United States International Trade Commission estimated that ATPA helped to expand job opportunities in the flower and asparagus industries, particularly to individuals who otherwise might have engaged in illicit drug crop production and related activities.[63] After ATPA was amended to include textile and apparel articles, all four countries experienced related output and employment growth, particularly in Peru and Colombia. The textile and apparel sectors have been a source of legitimate economic activity and employment in some Andean regions. Industry representatives there are concerned about losing ATPA preferences because of the importance of the United States as an export market. The removal of Bolivia as a designated ATPA beneficiary amidst political uncertainty has likely affected the potential for long-term investment in Bolivia, which may, in turn, have contributed to volatility in Bolivia's FDI flows as well as potential ATPA-related investment.[64]

AGOA preferences, combined with macroeconomic reforms, played a positive role in economic growth in sub-Saharan Africa in some industry sectors. For example, footwear exports from the region grew 33% overall between 2002 and 2006 as a result of duty-free access to the U.S. market under AGOA.[65] At the same time, African exports continue to be the least diversified of all developing regions, and many African economies still remain vulnerable to external shocks caused by reliance on primary commodity exports such as oil.[66]

Comparative Advantage and Development

While preferences may lead to important gains in manufacturing growth in some sectors and countries, a critical question is whether they help a country exploit a comparative advantage in trade, or artificially induce investment in industries that otherwise would be uncompetitive in the global market place. Some evidence points to support for comparative advantage in many cases where preferences build on an existing or nascent industry, allowing firms to gain a foothold in the international marketplace.[67] Preferences appear to have provided an opportunity for some of the current emerging markets such as India and Brazil to expand their international reach in certain markets. For example, India's utilization rate of the GSP program is very high (about 83%)[68]—spurred on, in part, by jewelry exports. The incentives created through the ATPA program may also have played a role in the expansion of the flower industry in Colombia and Ecuador. According to the Society of American Florists, about 67% of fresh flowers (as sold by dollar volume) in the United States are imports, with Colombia and Ecuador as the top two exporters. Apparel is an important sector for expanding export diversification in developing countries, particularly those with liberal rules of origin.[69] Countries such as Haiti have benefitted significantly from flexible rules of origin for apparel goods.

On the other hand, some countries may be encouraged by preferential programs to develop industry sectors in which they would otherwise not be able to compete, diverting public and private investment fro other uses. Supply constraints and difficult business environments can overcome any benefit that tariff preferences may offer.[70]

Export Diversification

Trade preference programs are unlikely to help poor countries achieve their development goals unless there is some transformation in their export structure away from primary goods.[71] USTR officials argue, for example, that AGOA is helping to expand and diversify trade between the United States and sub-Saharan Africa by building partnerships between U.S. and African businesses.[72] According to a 2009 report by the International Trade Administration, U.S. imports under AGOA are becoming increasingly diverse. Some of the more significant growth is taking place in jewelry and jewelry parts, fruit and nut products, fruit juices, leather products, plastic products, and cocoa paste. Apparel production has also benefitted.[73]

Because sub-Saharan Africa's preferential trade with the world still largely consists of oil and petroleum products, however, points to the crux of the diversification problem. With petroleum accounting for 93% of AGOA trade, the program may not be having the desired effect on Africa's economic development.[74] Such a case argues for aid in helping countries in Africa to take fuller advantage of the benefits that trade preferences offer and perhaps for reconsideration of programs incentives.

Preference Erosion

Preference erosion refers to the diminishing of the preference margin because tariff levels are being reduced in either multilateral or reciprocal bilateral or regional trade agreements. As tariffs fall worldwide, the benefit of zero tariffs in preference programs becomes smaller. It is an important point in the Doha Round negotiations from LDC perspectives. Particularly affected are countries participating in preference programs that cover most of their trade. There is a disincentive for LDCs to support multilateral trade liberalization should it result in reducing the benefits of their preference programs.[75] Products that otherwise face relatively high tariffs, such as apparel, are also subject to relatively greater preference erosion. One study cites apparel producing countries Cape Verde, Haiti, Malawi, Mauritania, and Sao Tome and Principe as the most vulnerable to preference erosion.[76]

Given there has not been a multilateral agreement under the WTO since the 1994 Uruguay Round, most preference erosion has occurred because of the expanding bilateral and regional trade agreements, and the 2005 WTO Agreement on Textiles and Clothing (ATC), which eliminated quantitative export restrictions and import quotas.[77] Under these circumstances, developing countries see the Doha Round as a continuation of trends that reduce their preference benefits. There is broad agreement, however, that in the aggregate, preference erosion is quantitatively small relative to the global benefits of MFN trade liberalization, although for certain countries it may be costly.[78]

Country Usage Concentration

While U.S. preference programs are open to many countries (for example, there are over 130 GSP beneficiaries), actual preference usage seems to be highly concentrated in only a few countries. In 2006, the top 25 preference beneficiaries accounted for 95 percent of U.S. preference imports.[79] As part of the debate over preference programs, some discussion has gravitated toward reconsidering their design in ways that would broaden their use, particularly by LDCs that may not be endowed with energy exports or have limited capability to develop apparel manufacturing.

Eligibility Issues

Trade preferences, by their nature, divide countries into two camps: those who receive them and those that do not. This dichotomy raises some political issues that affect attitudes toward preference programs. Countries that have preferential access to developed economies want to maintain that advantage. They do this by advocating for precluding the extension of preferences to other countries. Large developing countries also lobby to ensure that their continued benefit is not jeopardized by a change in graduation or other rules that might reduce their eligibility.

For example, some AGOA beneficiaries have expressed concern that proposals to extend DFQF access to all LDCs (including apparel exporters Bangladesh and Cambodia) will place Africa's developing apparel industries in direct competition with these countries for U.S. market share, thereby eroding the preferences they currently exclusively enjoy. Some Members have sought an overhaul of preference programs to make it easier to graduate "advanced" developing countries such as India and Brazil from the GSP because of their opposition of U.S. interests in DDA negotiations.[80] Others in the academic world have also pointed to the benefits of focusing preference programs exclusively on the poorest of the developing countries.[81]

A second issue involves the opportunity costs of eligibility criteria. All U.S. programs, for example, require participating countries to meet numerous non-trade related criteria. These range from adopting labor commitments to ensuring assistance is forthcoming on drug interdiction, among other policies. While the United States readily acknowledges that these foreign policy concerns are part of their preference programs, they represent opportunity costs to the recipient country that some argue amounts to "politicizing trade."[82]

Effects on the U.S. Market

The United States potentially faces costs in permitting unilateral trade preferences to developing countries. Domestic industries may face greater import competition as lower-cost imports enter the U.S. market, which could affect production, employment, and wages. However, preference programs are designed to limit the economic impact on domestic producers by various means.

In the GSP, U.S. import-competing manufacturers are largely protected from severe economic impact by three features. First, some products, such as most textile and apparel goods, are designated "import sensitive" and are therefore ineligible for duty-free treatment.[83] Second, "competitive need limits" in the GSP are triggered if imports of a product reach a certain threshold.[84] Third, U.S. producers may petition the United States Trade Representative (USTR) that GSP treatment granted to eligible articles be withdrawn. These petitions are considered during the annual review of the GSP program.[85]

Although the smaller regional preference programs include preferences for additional "import-sensitive" products, such as textiles and apparel, these differences do not greatly increase the potential for significant negative effects on U.S. producers. First, tariff lines given duty-free access can be very narrowly tailored to mitigate the impact of the preferences. Second, rules of origin are often carefully written to minimize effects on domestic producers. For example, for apparel imported from an AGOA country to receive the AGOA preference, no more than 10% (by weight) of the fiber and yarns making up the product can originate in a country other than the AGOA beneficiary or the United States.[86] Some U.S. apparel producers actually benefit from preferences through an integrated value-added chain of production between the U.S. producers and those in Central America and the Caribbean, which lowers their overall costs relative to other major global producers, such as those in China.[87] These cost factors have also assisted U.S. producers in retaining U.S. market share that could have been lost to Asian producers following the expiration of the WTO Agreement on Textiles and Clothing on January 1, 2005.[88]

Also in terms of U.S. benefits, some U.S. manufacturers who use imported inputs benefit from the lower cost of the intermediate manufactured goods and raw materials imported under preference programs.[89] U.S. demand for certain individual products, such as jewelry, leather, and aluminum, is also quite significant. Ultimately, consumers also benefit from the lower prices of products imported duty-free under preference programs.[90]

Even though preferences are structured to minimize the impact on U.S. producers, some amount of injury does occur. For example, the U.S. International Trade Commission found that U.S. growers of asparagus, fresh cut roses, chrysanthemums, carnations, and anthuriums may have experienced displacement of more than 5% of the value of production in 2005 because of imports that receive the ATPA preference.[91]

With regard to losses in tariff revenues, over time, most of these costs have been shown to be relatively small. For example, CBO estimated that P.L. 111-124, which renewed the ATPA and GSP until December 31, 2010, amounted to a loss of revenue of $589 million in FY2010 and $196 million in FY2011.[92] Imports entering duty-free are also relatively small compared to the total dollar value of imports to the United States.

Overall effects on the U.S. economy are quite small. For example, the value of goods imported under the GSP program in 2008 represented only about $31.7 billion, compared to total U.S. imports of $2.1 trillion. Imports from all preference programs amounted to only about 5.2% of all U.S. trade (see *Figure 2*).[93]

LEGISLATIVE OPTIONS FOR CONGRESS

The debate in Congress over trade preferences encompasses multiple viewpoints. Leaving the programs largely as they are is one. Others see the need for revision to address specific problems.

These include: (1) the role that preferences may play as a disincentive for beneficiary countries, particularly large developing countries, to embrace fully the Doha Round of multilateral trade negotiations;[94] (2) problems of compliance with eligibility criteria;[95] (3) the need to press for reciprocal trade treatments as poor countries reach a certain level of development; and (4) the need to focus them more on the least developed countries.[96] Policy discussions tend to revolve around five basic program parameters: (1) renewal period, (2) harmonization, (3) country coverage, (4) product coverage, and (5) eligibility criteria.

Renewal Period

With the exception of CBERA, all preference programs are time-limited and Congress must reauthorize them if they are to continue. Although Congress has generally viewed these programs as temporary, it has historically chosen to renew them, usually without interruption and often with broad approval. Program beneficiaries, including governments, importers, and consuming industries, advocate diligently for continued program support.

The primary argument for longer-term renewals is to establish a predictable trade environment that will attract long-term investment. Preferences translate into relatively lower costs of goods imported into the United States, which provide businesses with the incentive to operate in otherwise less competitive or desirable locations. Investors are more likely to consider long-term commitments when preferences are not subject to repeated short-term extensions, which adds an element of uncertainty to business planning, and also has implications for employment and economic stability in beneficiary countries. Extended preference horizons also support development of stable sourcing relationships and improved working environments given the emphasis eligibility criteria places on such factors as rule of law, good business practices, and worker rights.[97] Some Members, though, view extended renewal as conditioned on other program changes such as those discussed below.[98]

The 111th Congress has already acted to extend some preference programs. In the first session, it provided a one-year extension for the GSP and ATPA through December 31, 2010 (P.L. 111-124). In the second session, the HELP Act (P.L. 111-117) extended the CBTPA and Haiti HOPE Act through September 30, 2020. If Congress takes up comprehensive legislation, it is possible that it may consider the costs and benefits of harmonizing renewal periods and perhaps act to lengthen the renewal period for GSP and ATPA.

Harmonization

Preference programs have similar, but not identical, program features. A key theme for renewal has been to review these policy parameters to determine if there are opportunities to simplify, harmonize, and make more consistent program features such as eligibility criteria, rules of origin, and product coverage. Some areas may be easier to harmonize than others. For example, it may be possible to standardize eligibility criteria across all programs.

Harmonizing the complex "maze" of rules of origin could be a much greater challenge. Still, many view this as an important step toward making the programs operate more efficiently, not only from the perspective of businesses attempting to meet these rules, but also at the U.S. border where customs officials must determine the eligibility of each product entering the country. Because these rules were carefully crafted to maximize benefits to the intended countries, while minimizing any adverse effects on U.S. producers and preventing transshipment, harmonization may prove challenging to achieve in practice.[99]

Trade capacity building (TCB), or training to improve the capability of firms in beneficiary countries to use these preferences, may provide a partial solution. The Government Accountability Office (GAO) has reported that research on the textile and apparel inputs industry in sub-Saharan Africa has confirmed that TCB is key to improvement of the competitiveness of the sector and utilization of preferences.[100]

Country Coverage

Although preference program legislation gives the President the authority to determine country eligibility based on designated criteria, Congress specifically designates overall which countries may receive the preferences. For example, Congress designated 48 sub-Saharan African countries as potentially eligible to receive the AGOA preference, but the President initially designated 34 countries as eligible based on the criteria Congress set forth in the statute.[101] Congress could legislatively expand or contract country coverage at any time. For example, several bills in Congress seek specifically to prevent Vietnam from obtaining GSP status due to its poor record on worker rights.[102]

By definition, trade preferences are targeted toward developing countries, but there are different opinions regarding how broadly they should apply. Some argue that they should be targeted only toward LDCs that need them most.[103] Higher or "middle" income developing countries resist this approach.

Congress could also expand regional programs or create new preference programs in order to incorporate those LDCs not currently covered in AGOA or the other regional programs. Three bills introduced in the 111th Congress (H.R. 1837, S. 1665, and S. 780) would expand coverage in the ATPA to include Paraguay and/or Uruguay. The Tariff Relief Assistance for Developing Economies Act of 2009 (S. 1141) would authorize extending AGOA-like trade preferences for textile and apparel goods to non-African LDCs, including Afghanistan, Bangladesh, Bhutan, Cambodia, Kiribati, Lao People's Democratic Republic, Maldives, Nepal, Samoa, Solomon Islands, Timor-Leste (East Timor), Tuvalu, Vanuatu, and Yemen. The bill would also extend product coverage for these countries to other "import-sensitive" items, subject to International Trade Commission (ITC) recommendation and Presidential determination.

Another approach would be to reduce coverage for advanced developing countries, or require more reciprocity from these nations.[104] Decreasing the number of country participants could also be achieved by applying mandatory country "graduation" to all preference programs, such as currently implemented in the GSP. According to the GSP statute, mandatory graduation occurs when a beneficiary country is determined to be a "high income country" as defined by official International Bank for Reconstruction and Development (World Bank) statistics.[105] Alternatively, Congress could choose another measure of income for graduation from preference programs, or require that country graduation be determined by a comprehensive review of its industries and economy.[106]

One bill—the New Partnership for Trade Development Act of 2009 (S. 4101)—seeks to expand country coverage in textiles and apparel to more LDCs, while limiting the imports of more competitive countries. The legislation would amend the AGOA and GSP programs to expand preferences for LDCs, while strengthening and improving benefits to AGOA countries to ensure that existing African beneficiaries would not be negatively affected.[107] The bill would strengthen AGOA preferences by granting DFQF treatment to all least-developed AGOA countries; applying the GSP 35% value-added rules, and extending the third-country fabric provision until September 30,

2015.[108] It would also extend DFQF benefits to additional eligible non-African LDCs. For those countries that are already "significant apparel suppliers" to the United States,[109] the bill would limit apparel imports eligible for preferences. The bill would also allow extension of coverage to articles deemed "import-sensitive" with respect to the GSP under certain conditions. The bill would require a transparent decision-making process regarding GSP competitive need limit waivers. The bill would continue to extend benefits to "upper-middle income" GSP beneficiaries, provided that they, in turn, grant trade preferences to LDCs and sub-Saharan African countries.

Eligibility Criteria

Some importers and non-governmental organizations (NGOs) advocate amending preference program eligibility criteria so that they are "clear, commercially meaningful, and achievable."[110] Proponents of this view tend to differ in their selection of criteria, however. For example, some NGO advocates object to conditions requiring protection of intellectual property on the grounds that the application of these criteria can be "arbitrary and unpredictable."[111] Business proponents, however, might be more favorable to inclusion of intellectual property eligibility criteria on the grounds that such protections help them to preserve the value of their products.

An alternative might be to reconstitute preference programs to include incentives to beneficiaries other than tariff reductions, or to create an additional preference program for countries that are willing to comply with additional U.S. objectives. The European Union, for example, has crafted a "GSP-plus" program that offers additional product coverage to particularly vulnerable developing countries, provided that they have ratified and implemented a number of core international conventions on human rights, labor rights, good governance and environmental protection.[112]

Product Coverage

Congress could re-evaluate current product coverage, and decide to expand or eliminate certain products from preference programs. For example preference advocates argue that immediate DFQF could be extended to all LDCs with minimal effects on the U.S. economy.[113]

No U.S. preference program as currently authorized provides complete DFQF access. For example, some U.S. products, such as certain apparel, leather, electronics, steel, and glass products, are deemed "import-sensitive" in GSP due to possible negative effects on U.S. domestic producers. In terms of DFQF access for textiles and ready-made apparel products, the AGOA program is the broadest, although significant restrictions are still in place (i.e., caps are placed on use of yarns and fabrics that are of third-country or sub-Saharan African origin).

As part of the World Trade Organization (WTO) Doha Round negotiations, the United States and other developed country WTO members and "developing country members declaring themselves in a position to do so" agreed to provide DFQF access, but these commitments will not take effect until (or unless) the Doha Round is completed.[114]

Some in Congress favor expanding product coverage in preference programs. For example, several bills in the 111th Congress seek to expand AGOA-like textile and apparel benefits to other non-African LDCs—a move that some African countries oppose due to concerns that they would be put at a disadvantage compared to LDCs like Cambodia and Bangladesh that have sophisticated, established apparel industries already in place.[115]

If Congress chose to expand or harmonize product coverage, it could also shield import-competing U.S. industries by applying an across-the-board cap on preferential access. For example, the CNL thresholds that apply in GSP (discussed above) could be implemented in all programs, or be enacted in a harmonized program. Congress could also provide tariff reductions (as opposed to duty-free access) for certain "import-sensitive" products in all U.S. preference programs as currently implemented. This approach is similar to the Australian GSP program, which provides a 5% preference margin on products with tariffs over 5%, rather than strictly duty-free access.[116]

Preferences also differ with regard to cumulation, which allows for combining inputs from numerous beneficiary countries under one or more preference programs as long as a substantial transformation still occurs in the beneficiary country. For example, one of the requirements for apparel articles to qualify for the ATPA states that they may be sewn or assembled in one *or more* ATPA beneficiary countries or the United States. In the GSP, certain pre-designated regional groups may meet the value-added requirement by combining (cumulating) inputs in order to qualify for preferential access. The Haiti HOPE Act provisions also allow for regional cumulation and limited use of third-party materials. Allowing LDC beneficiaries to "cumulate" inputs from all developing countries could provide flexibility and could have the added effect of simplifying rules of origin.[117] Congress could restrict or expand the availability of preferences by modifying these provisions to include a greater or lesser percentage of inputs from other beneficiary countries, or by permitting a larger percentage of third-party inputs.

OUTLOOK

The 111th Congress has held hearings on trade preference programs in both the House and Senate, where some Members expressed interest in amending and harmonizing some of the preferences provisions. As specialized programs intended to serve as a form of assistance to developing countries, program design is critical in determining whether those countries most in need are being well served. Because these are complex programs with multiple design features, evaluating them is a challenging and complicated exercise. If the 111th Congress does not take up legislation that would reform preference programs, the issue will likely continue to be prominent in the 112th Congress.

APPENDIX. ELIGIBLE COUNTRIES AND PRODUCTS IMPORTED BY PREFERENCE PROGRAM

Table A-1. Eligible Countries by Preference Program (Least-Developed Countries (LDCs) in Italics)

Designated Beneficiary Countries	Generalized System of Preferences (GSP)	Caribbean Basin Economic Recovery Act (CBERA)	Caribbean Basin Trade Partnership Act of 2000 (CBTPA)	Andean Trade Preference Act (ATPA)	African Growth and Opportunity Act (AGOA)
Afghanistan	X				
Angola	X				X
Antigua and Barbuda		X			
Argentina	X				
Armenia	X				
Aruba		X			
Azerbaijan	X				
Bahamas		X			
Bangladesh	X				
Barbados		X	X		
Belize	X	X	X		

Benin	X				X
Bhutan	X				
Bolivia	X				
Bosnia and Hercegovina	X				
Botswana	X				X
Brazil	X				
Burkina Faso	X				X
Burundi	X				X
Designated Beneficiary Countries	Generalized System of Preferences (GSP)	Caribbean Basin Economic Recovery Act (CBERA)	Caribbean Basin Trade Partnership Act of 2000 (CBTPA)	Andean Trade Preference Act (ATPA)	African Growth and Opportunity Act (AGOA)
Cambodia	X				
Cameroon	X				X
Cape Verde	X				X
Central African Republic	X				
Chad	X				X
Colombia	X			X	
Comoros	X				X
Congo (Brazzaville)	X				X
Congo (Kinshasa)	X				X
Cote d'Ivoire	X				
Croatia	X				
Djibouti	X				X
Dominica	X	X			
East Timor	X				
Ecuador	X			X	
Egypt	X				
Equatorial Guinea	X				
Eritrea	X				
Ethiopia	X				X
Fiji	X				
Gabon	X				X
Gambia, The	X				X
Georgia	X				
Ghana	X				X
Grenada	X	X			
Guinea	X				

Table A-1. (Continued).

Designated Beneficiary Countries	Generalized System of Preferences (GSP)	Caribbean Basin Economic Recovery Act (CBERA)	Caribbean Basin Trade Partnership Act of 2000 (CBTPA)	Andean Trade Preference Act (ATPA)	African Growth and Opportunity Act (AGOA)
Guinea-Bissau	X				X
Guyana	X	X	X		
Haiti	X	X	X		
India	X				
Indonesia	X				
Iraq	X				
Jamaica	X	X	X		
Jordan	X				
Kazakhstan	X				
Kenya	X				X
Kiribati	X				
Kosovo	X				
Kyrgyzstan	X				
Lebanon	X				
Lesotho	X				X
Liberia	X				X
Macedonia	X				
Madagascar	X				
Malawi	X				X
Maldives	X				
Mali	X				X
Mauritania	X				X
Mauritius	X				X
Moldova	X				
Mongolia	X				
Montenegro	X				
Montserrat		X			
Mozambique	X				X
Namibia	X				X
Nepal	X				
Netherlands Antilles		X			
Niger	X				
Federal Republic of Nigeria					X
Pakistan	X				
Panama	X	X	X		
Papua New Guinea	X				
Paraguay	X				

Peru				X	
Philippines	X				
Russia	X				
Rwanda	X				X
Saint Lucia	X	X	X		
Samoa	X				
Sao Tome and Principe	X				X
Senegal	X				X
Serbia	X				
Seychelles	X				X
Sierra Leone	X				X
Solomon Islands	X				
Somalia	X				
South Africa	X				X
Sri Lanka	X				
St. Kitts/Nevis	X	X			
St. Vincent and the Grenadines	X	X			
Suriname	X				
Swaziland	X				X
Tanzania	X				X
Thailand	X				
Togo	X				X
Tonga	X				
Trinidad and Tobago		X	X		
Tunisia	X				
Turkey	X				
Tuvalu	X				
Uganda	X				X
Ukraine	X				
Uruguay	X				
Uzbekistan	X				
Vanuatu	X				
Venezuela	X				
Virgin Islands, British		X			
Yemen	X				
Zambia	X				X
Zimbabwe	X				

Source: Harmonized Tariff Schedule of the United States (HTSUS) Revision 1, July 1, 2010. See General Notes 4, 7, 16, and 17 for definitive country listings.

Notes: GSP Independent Countries only. See HTSUS General Note 4 for a listing of Non-Independent Countries and Territories, and Associations of Countries that are treated as one country for purposes of the GSP. LDCs are designated as such for purposes of the GSP and receive duty-free access to additional tariff lines.

Table A-2. Major U.S. Imports by Preference Program

Top 15 U.S. Imports under the Generalized System of Preferences (GSP), 2008	
HTS Subheading and Description	Actual U.S. Dollars
27090020 - Petroleum oils and oils from bituminous minerals, crude, testing 25 degrees A.P.I. or more (LDC only)	9,740,681,021
27090010 - Petroleum oils and oils from bituminous minerals, crude, testing under 25 degrees A.P.I. (LDC only)	1,024,288,176
71121150 - Silver articles of jewelry and parts thereof, not elsewhere specified, valued over $18 per dozen pieces or parts	481,322,767
71131929 - Gold necklaces and neck chains	381,788,293
40111010 - New pneumatic radial tires, of rubber, of a kind used on motor cars	379,467,478
76061230 – Aluminum alloy, plates/sheets/strip	339,609,297
71131950 - Precious metal (other than silver) articles of jewelry and parts thereof, whether or not plated or clad with precious metal, not elsewhere specified	322,809,325
39076000 – Polyethylene terephthalate in primary forms	253,278,318
40112010 - New pneumatic radial tires, of rubber, of a kind used on buses or trucks	207,368,571
21069099 - Food preparations not elsewhere specified or included, not canned or frozen	165,198,981
68029900 - Monumental or building stone & arts. thereof, further worked than simply cut/sawn, not elsewhere specified	154,998,583
40151910 – Seamless gloves of vulcanized rubber other than hard rubber, other than surgical or medical gloves	140,171,668
90015000 – Spectacle lenses of materials other than glass, unmounted	118,288,524
85042300 - Liquid dielectric transformers having a power handling capacity exceeding 10,000 kVA	108,983,792
17011110 - Cane sugar, raw, in solid form, without added flavoring or coloring	89,661,957
Subtotal - GSP Imports Above:	13,907,916,751
All Other:	17,754,837,014
Total GSP Imports:	31,662,753,765

Top 15 U.S. Imports under the Caribbean Basin Economic Recovery Act (CBERA), 2008	
HTS Subheading and Description	Actual U.S. Dollars
29851120 – Methanol (Methyl alcohol), other than imported only for use in producing synthetic natural gas (SNG) or for direct use as fuel	1,175,154,686
22071060 - Undenatured ethyl alcohol of 80% by volume alcohol or higher, for non-beverage purposes	483,063,905
08043040 - Pineapples, fresh or dried, not reduced in size, in crates or other packages	393,122,221
39031100 - Polystyrene, expandable, in primary forms	135,521,790
20091100 - Orange juice, frozen, unfermented and not containing added spirits	64,689,149
07149020 - Fresh or chilled yams, whether or not sliced or in the form of pellets	29,915,488
71081250 - Gold, nonmonetary, unwrought	26,890,097
17011110 - Cane sugar, raw, in solid form, without added flavoring or coloring	22,300,311
22072000 - Ethyl alcohol and other spirits, denatured, of any strength	20,003,309
08072000 - Papayas (papaws), fresh	14,048,666
16041440 - Tunas and skipjack, not in airtight containers, not in oil, in bulk or in immediate containers weighing with contents over 6.8 kg each	12,925,254
22071030 - Undenatured ethyl alcohol of 80 % by volume of alcohol or higher, for beverage purposes	8,685,447
85291020 - Television antennas and antenna reflectors, and parts suitable for use therewith	7,652,688
08045040 - Guavas, mangoes, and mangosteens, fresh, if entered during the period September 1 through May 31, inclusive	5,173,035
22029090 - Nonalcoholic beverages, not elsewhere specified not including fruit or vegetable juices of heading 2009	4,226,852
Subtotal - Total CBERA Products Above:	2,403,372,898
All Other:	619,158,293
Total CBERA Imports:	3,022,531,191

Table A-2. (Continued)

Top 15 U.S. Imports under the Caribbean Basin Trade Partnership Act (CBTPA), 2008	
HTS Subheading and Description	Actual U.S. Dollars
27099920 - Petroleum oils and oils from bituminous minerals, crude, testing 25 degrees A.P.I. or more	903,985,774
61091000 - T-shirts, singlets, tank tops and similar garments, knitted or crocheted, of cotton	168,910,180
61102020 – Sweaters, pullovers and similar articles, knitted or crocheted, of cotton, not elsewhere specified	145,801,021
27101125 – Naphthas (excluding motor fuel/motor fuel blended stock) from petroleum oils & bituminous minerals (o/than crude)	143,644,824
62034240 -Men's or boys' trousers and shorts, not bibs, not knitted or crocheted, of cotton, not containing 15% or more by weight of down	50,873,428
61099010 - T-shirts, singlets, tank tops and similar garments, knitted or crocheted, of man-made fibers	22,106,139
27101905 -Distillate and residual fuel oil (including blends) derived from petroleum or oils from bituminous minerals, testing under 25 degrees A.P.I.	19,571,420
62034340 - Men's or boys' trousers, breeches & shorts, of synthetic fibers, containing under 15% weight down, and containing under 36% weight wool, not water resistant	19,062,093
27101145 -Light oil mixtures of hydrocarbons from petroleum oils & bituminous minerals(other than crude)	15,073,275
62053020 -Men's or boys' shirts, not knitted or crocheted, of manmade fibers, not elsewhere specified	6,224,233
16041430 - Tunas and skipjack, not in oil, in airtight containers, not over 7 kg, not a product of U.S. possessions, over quota	2,555,140
61081100 -Women's or girls' slips and petticoats, knitted or crocheted, of man-made fibers	1,660,626
61143020 – Bodysuits and bodyshirts, knitted or crocheted, of man-made fibers	1,321,716
27101930 -Lubricating oils, with or without additives, from petroleum oils and bituminous minerals (o/than crude)	603,007
61012000 -Men's or boys' overcoats, carcoats, capes, cloaks, anoraks, windbreakers and similar articles, knitted or crocheted, of cotton	289,819
Total CBTPA Items Above:	1,501,682,695
All other CBTPA:	199,886,135
Total CBTPA Imports:	1,701,568,830

Top 15 U.S. Imports under the Andean Trade Preference Act (ATPA), 2008	
HTS Subheading and Description	Actual U.S. Dollars
27090010 - Petroleum oils and oils from bituminous minerals, crude, testing under 25 degrees A.P.I.	10,128,076,615
27090020 - Petroleum oils and oils from bituminous minerals, crude, testing 25 degrees A.P.I. or more	2,078,529,699
74031100 - Refined copper cathodes and sections of cathodes	844,388,290
27101905 – Distillate and residual fuel oil (including blends) derived from petroleum or oils from bituminous minerals, testing under 25 degrees A.P.I.	628,662,292
27101125 -Naphthas (except motor fuel/motor fuel blended stock) from petroleum oils & bituminous minerals (other than crude)	377,140,870
06031100 - Sweetheart, Spray and other Roses, fresh cut	310,291,331
61102020 - Sweaters, pullovers and similar articles, knitted or crocheted, of cotton, not elsewhere specified	239,924,774
06031900 - fresh cut, Anthuriums, Alstroemeria, Gypsophilia, Lilies, Snapdragons and flowers, not elsewhere specified	192,515,808
61051000 – Men's or boys' shirts, knitted or crocheted, of cotton	176,191,218
61091000 - T-shirts, singlets, tank tops and similar garments, knitted or crocheted, of cotton	162,482,114
7092090 - Asparagus, not elsewhere specified, fresh or chilled	145,195,953
62034240 -Men's or boys' trousers and shorts, not bibs, not knitted or crocheted, of cotton, not containing 15% or more by weight of down	85,840,968
16041430 - Tunas and skipjack, not in oil, in airtight containers, not over 7 kg, not a product of U.S. possessions, over quota	70,067,275
06034240 -Chrysanthemums, fresh cut	66,942,147
06031270 - Other Carnations, fresh cut	37,759,897
Subtotal -All ATPA Items Above:	15,544,009,251
All Other:	1,698,665,706
Total ATPA Imports:	17,242,674,957

Table A-2. (Continued)

Top 15 U.S. Imports under the African Growth and Opportunity Act (AGOA), 2008	
HTS Subheading and Description	Actual U.S. Dollars
27090020 - Petroleum oils and oils from bituminous minerals, crude, testing 25 degrees A.P.I. or more	48,518,019,968
27090010 - Petroleum oils from bituminous minerals testing under 25 degrees A.P.I.	2,731,811,660
87032300 -Motor cars & other motor vehicles for transport of persons, with spark-ignition internal combustion reciprocal piston engine with cylinder capacity of 1500 cc and not more than 3000 cc	1,553,389,022
27101905 - Distillate and residual fuel oil (including blends) derived from petroleum or oils from bituminous minerals, testing under 25 degrees A.P.I.	750,982,539
27101125 -Naphthas (except motor fuel/motor fuel blended stock) from petroleum oils & bituminous minerals (other than crude)	658,853,842
72021150 - Ferromanganese containing by weight more than 4 % carbon	367,406,195
62046240 -Women's or girls' trousers, breeches and shorts, not knitted or crocheted, of cotton, not elsewhere specified	256,791,659
87032400 -Motor cars & other motor vehicles for transport of persons, with spark internal combustion reciprocating piston engine with cylinder capacity of 3000 cc.	250,978,213
61102020 -Sweaters, pullovers and similar articles, knitted or crocheted, of cotton, not elsewhere specified	161,602,238
62034240 -Men's or boys' trousers and shorts, not bibs, not knitted or crocheted, of cotton, not containing 15% or more by weight of down	152,706,522
62052020 -Men's or boys' shirts, not knitted or crocheted, of cotton, not elsewhere specified	81,008,135
61103030 - Sweaters, pullovers and similar articles, knitted or crocheted, of manmade fibers, not elsewhere specified	75,623,601
38237060 -Industrial fatty alcohols other than derived from fatty substances of animal or vegetable origin	73,833,844
61046220 -Women's or girls' trousers, breeches and shorts, knitted or crocheted, of cotton	73,810,107
27101145 -Light oil mixtures of hydrocarbons from petroleum oils & bituminous minerals(other than crude) or preparations 70% or more by weight from petroleum oils, not elsewhere specified	50,463,377
Subtotal -AGOA Imports Above:	55,757,280,922
All Other:	616,369,979
Total AGOA Imports:	56,373,650,901

Source: Harmonized Tariff Schedule of the United States (HTSUS); International Trade Commission Trade Dataweb, http://dataweb.usitc.gov.

End Notes

[1] In the United States MFN treatment is defined in law as normal trade relations (NTR).

[2] The terms of trade or the ratio of export prices to import prices tends to fall with commodity prices over the long run, causing deteriorated trade and current account positions.

[3] Bernard Hoekman, Will Martin, and Carlos A. Primo Braga, "Quantifying the Value of Preferences and Potential Erosion Losses," in *Trade Preference Erosion: Measurement and Policy Response*, ed. Bernard Hoekman, Will Martin, and Carlos A. Primo Braga (New York: Palgrave MacMillan, 2009), pp. 1-2.

[4] U.S. Congress, House, Committee on Ways and Means, Subcommittee on Foreign Trade, "Hearing on the Operation, Impact, and Future of the U.S. Preference Programs," Hearing Advisory, November 10, 2009.

[5] According to the GSP statute (see 19 U.S.C. § 2467) beneficiary and least-developed beneficiary countries must be designated as such by Executive Order or Presidential Proclamation. Least-developed beneficiaries are designated according to the same eligibility criteria as beneficiary developing countries and must comply with the same requirements, but receive tariff benefits on additional products.

[6] 19 U.S.C. §§ 2461-2467, as amended. For a more complete description of the GSP, see CRS Report RL33663, *Generalized System of Preferences: Background and Renewal Debate*, by Vivian C. Jones.

[7] 19 U.S.C. § 2462.

[8] Ibid.

[9] 19 U.S.C. § 2463(a)(2).

[10] 19 U.S.C.§ 2463(b).

[11] 19 U.S.C.§ 2463(c). If a CNL is in place on a product, an interested party from a beneficiary country can request redesignation of the product's eligibility if imports of the product fall below the CNL limits in a subsequent year.

[12] 19 U.S.C. § 2462(e). The last countries graduated from the GSP were Equatorial Guinea and Croatia (effective January 1, 2011) because the President determined that they had become "high income" countries. See Proclamation 8467 of December 23, 2009, *To Modify Duty-Free Treatment Under the Generalized System of Preferences, and for Other Purposes,* 74 *Federal Register* 69221. The per capita GNP limit is set at the lower bound of the World Bank's definition of a "high income" country which was $11,116 in 2006 (see USTR, Generalized System of Preferences Guidebook).

[13] 19 U.S.C. § 2462(c)(2).

[14] P.L. 98-67, 19 U.S.C. § 2701ff.

[15] P.L. 101-382. For more background, see CRS Report RL33951, *U.S. Trade Policy and the Caribbean: From Trade Preferences to Free Trade Agreements*, by J. F. Hornbeck.

[16] P.L. 106-200, Title III, 19 U.S.C. §2703.

[17] P.L. 111-171. See CRS Report RL34687, *The Haitian Economy and the HOPE Act*, by J. F. Hornbeck.

[18] P.L. 109-53, 19 U.S.C. § 4001 ff.

[19] Others include the Dominican Republic, El Salvador, Guatemala, Honduras, and Nicaragua.

[20] P.L. 109-432, 19 U.S.C. 2703a.

[21] P.L. 110-246, Subtitle D, Part I.

[22] CRS Report RL34687, *The Haitian Economy and the HOPE Act*, by J. F. Hornbeck.

[23] Title II of P.L. 102-182, 19 U.S.C. § 3201ff, most recently extended by P.L. 111-124.

[24] Title XXXI of P.L. 107-210.

[25] See P.L. 107-210, Div. C, Title XXXI, sec. 3102.

[26] Title I of P.L. 106-200 (19 U.S.C. § 3701 – 3741), as amended.

[27] P.L. 109-432, Div. D, Title VI, section 6004.

[28] 19 U.S.C. § 2466a (a)(1)(B).

[29] 19 U.S.C. § 3721.

[30] 19 U.S.C. § 3732(b). Office of the United States Trade Representative, *2008 Comprehensive Report on U.S. Trade and Investment Policy Toward Sub-Saharan Africa and Implementation of the African Growth and Opportunity Act: The Eighth of Eight Annual Reports*, May 2008, p. 47.

[31] 19 U.S.C. § 3703.

[32] CRS Report RS22183, *Trade Preferences for Developing Countries and the World Trade Organization (WTO)*, by Jeanne J. Grimmett.

[33] Ibid. The Enabling Clause replaced a 1974 GATT waiver on preferences under which the United States and other countries originally adopted and implemented preference programs.

[34] According to the United Nations Conference on Trade And Development (UNCTAD), there are currently 13 countries that offer GSP programs: Australia, Belarus, Bulgaria, Canada, Estonia, the European Union, Japan, New Zealand, Norway, Russia, Switzerland, and Turkey.

[35] Julia V. Sekkel, *Summary of Major Trade Preference Programs*, Center for Global Development, April 2009, p. 15.

[36] Sanchez Arnau, Juan C., *The Generalized System of Preferences and the World Trade Organization,* London: Cameron May, Ltd., 2002, p. 187.

[37] United Nations Conference on Trade and Development (UNCTAD), *Generalized System of Preferences on the Scheme of Australia*, UNCTAD Technical Cooperation Project on Market Access, Trade Laws and Preferences, June 2000 (INT/97/A06), p. 5, http://www.unctad.org/en/docs/itcdtsbmisc56_en.pdf. [38]European Council Regulation (EC) 416/2001.

[39] European Council Regulation (EC) 732/2008. See also the European Commission website, http://ec.europa.eu/trade

[40] World Trade Organization, Ministerial Declaration, Annex F, December 18, 2005, WT/MIN(05)/DEC.

[41] Ibid.

[42] CRS Report RL32060, *World Trade Organization Negotiations: The Doha Development Agenda*, by Ian F. Fergusson.

[43] U.S. Congress, House Committee on Ways and Means, *Hearing on the Operation, Impact, and Future of the U.S. Preference Programs*, 111th Cong., 1st sess., November 17, 2009, Testimony of Alan Han of Nien Hsing Textile.

[44] U.S. Government Accountability Office, *International Trade: U.S. Trade Preference Programs Provide Important Benefits, but a More Integrated Approach Would Better Ensure Programs Meet Shared Goals*, GAO-08-443, March 2008, p. 40, http://www.gao.gov.

[45] U.S. Congress, House Committee on Ways and Means, *Hearing on the Operation, Impact, and Future of the U.S. Preference Programs*, 111th Cong., 1st sess., November 17, 2009. Testimony of David Love, Senior Vice President and Chief Supply Chain Officer, Levi Strauss & Co.

[46] U.S. Government Accountability Office, *International Trade: U.S. Trade Preference Programs Provide Important Benefits, but a More Integrated Approach Would Better Ensure Programs Meet Shared Goals*, GAO-08-443, March 2008, p. 42, http://www.gao.gov.

[47] U.S. Congress, Senate Committee on Finance, *U.S. Preference Programs: How Well Do They Work?*, 110th Cong., 1st sess., May 16, 2007, S. Hrg. 110-650 (Washington: GPO, 2007) Statement of Meredith Broadbent, Assistant U.S. Trade Representative for Market Access and Telecommunications, Office of the U.S. Trade Representative, Washington, D.C., p. 4.

[48] Ibid.

[49] "The Real Record on Workers' Rights in Central America," AFL-CIO, April 2005, http://www.aflcio.org.

[50] U.S. Congress, House Committee on Ways and Means, *Hearing on the Operation, Impact, and Future of the U.S. Preference Programs*, 111th Cong., 1st sess., November 17, 2009, Testimony of David Hastings, chairman of the Mount Vernon Mills, on behalf of the National Council of Textile Organizations (NCTO).

[51] Caglar Ozden and Eric Reinhardt, *The Perversity of Preferences*: *The Generalized System of Preferences and Developing Country Trade Policies, 1976-2000*, The World Bank Development Research Group, Working Paper, January 2003, p. 2.

[52] The "real" preference margin is better calculated as the difference between the tariff preference on competing goods from other developing countries and the tariff preferences offered on goods from the country under study. [52] Hoekman, Martin, and Braga, op. cit., p. 4.

[53] Hoekman, Martin, and Braga, op. cit., p. 9.

[54] CRS Report RL33577, *U.S. International Trade: Trends and Forecasts*, by Dick K. Nanto and J. Michael Donnelly.

[55] While the WTO uses the term "most-favored-nation" to describe nondiscriminatory trade treatment, U.S. law since 1998 has referred to this treatment as "normal trade relations" (NTR) status. See P.L. 105-206, section 5003.

[56] World Trade Organization, "United States: Tariffs and Imports, Summary and Duty Ranges," http://stat.wto.org/TariffProfiles/US_e.htm.

[57] Hoekman, Martin, and Braga, op. cit., p.7.

[58] Ibid., pp. 4-6.

[59]As shown in Figure 1, U.S. imports from developing countries, including those entering under preference programs, fell dramatically in 2009 due to the global financial crisis. Therefore, we find that 2008 data may be more instructive than 2009 data when describing the economic effects of the various preference programs.

[60] CRS Report RL33663, *Generalized System of Preferences: Background and Renewal Debate*, by Vivian C. Jones.

[61] CRS Report RL33951, *U.S. Trade Policy and the Caribbean: From Trade Preferences to Free Trade Agreements*, by J. F. Hornbeck.

[62] CRS Report RL34687, *The Haitian Economy and the HOPE Act*, by J. F. Hornbeck.

[63] U.S. International Trade Commission, *Andean Trade Preference Act: Impact on U.S. Industries and Consumers, and on Drug Eradication and Crop Substitution*, Thirteenth Report, Investigation No. 332-352, Publication 4037, September 2008.

[64] For more information, see the following reports: USITC Publication 4037; *Confederacin de Empresarios Privados de Bolivia, The Importance of ATPDEA for Bolivia*, October 2008; and Université de Lausanne (Unil*), ATPDEA's End: Effects on Bolivian Real Incomes*, by Olivier Cadot, Etchel M. Fonseca, and Synabout Yaye Sakho, February 2008.

[65] United States International Trade Commission, *Sub-Saharan Africa: Factors Affecting Trade Patterns of Certain Industries*, Investigation Number 332-477, April 2008, http://www.usitc.gov/publications/332/pub3989.pdf.

[66] World Bank, World Trade Indicators 2008. South Africa is the most diversified economy on the continent, despite diversification efforts in many middle- and low-income African economies.

[67] See Raed Safadi and Ralph Latimore, eds., *Globalization and Emerging Economies: Brazil, Russia, India, Indonesia, China, South Africa*, Organization for International Cooperation and Development (OECD), 2008.

[68] CRS calculations based on U.S. International Trace Commission (USITC) trade statistics.

[69] Society of American Florists, *About the Flower Industry*, http://www.aboutflowers.com/about-the-flower-industry/industry-overview.html and Hoekman, Martin, and Braga, op. cit., pp. 21-22.

[70] Organization for International Cooperation and Development (OECD), *Making Open Markets Work for Development*, Policy Brief, October 2005, p. 2 and Ibid.

[71] OECD Secretary-General. The Generalized System of Preferences: Review of the First Decade. Organization of Economic Cooperation and Development, 1983, p. 9. CRS Report RL33663, *Generalized System of Preferences: Background and Renewal Debate*, by Vivian C. Jones.

[72] Office of the United States Trade Representative. "AGOA Opens Doors for U.S. Businesses," Press Release, August 5, 2010.

[73] Department of Commerce, International Trade Administration, "U.S.-African Trade Profile," p. 2, http://www.agoa.gov\ and Hoekman, Martin, and Braga, op. cit., pp. 21-22.

[74] "Trade: the U.S. and Sub-Saharan Africa: Oil is King," *Country Forecast Africa,* Economist Intelligence Unit, March 12, 2010; Kalley, Karanta, "Asia's Crude Oil Purchases from West Africa Rise Sharply in Q1," *Global Insight,* World Markets Research Center, March 8, 2010.

[75] Paul Brenton and Caglar Ozden, *Trade Preferences for Apparel and The Role of Rules of Origin – The Case of Africa*, The World Bank, p. 2.

[76] Hoekman, Martin, and Braga, op. cit., p. 18-19.

[77] Ibid.

[78] "NGOs, Business Groups Debate Principles for Preference Reform," *Inside U.S. Trade*, April 10, 2009, U.S. Government Accountability Office (GAO), *International Trade: U.S. Trade Preference Programs Provide Important Benefits, but a More Integrated Approach Would Better Ensure Programs Meet Shared Goals,* GAO-08-443, March 2008, p. 35, and Ibid., p.21.

[79] U.S. Government Accountability Office (GAO), *International Trade: U.S. Trade Preference Programs Provide Important Benefits, but a More Integrated Approach Would Better Ensure Programs Meet Shared Goals,* GAO-08-443, March 2008, p. 35.

[80] "Sen. Grassley Warns Brazil, India, on GSP; Stops Short of Predicting Graduation," Inside U.S. Trade, May 19, 2006. "Ways and Means Likely to Seek One-Year Extension of GSP, ATPDEA," *Inside U.S. Trade*, September 7, 2010.

[81] Paul Collier, *The Bottom Billion: Why the Poorest Countries Are Failing and What Can Be Done About It* (Oxford: Oxford University Press, 2007), pp. 168-169.

[82] For a summary, see Hoekman, Martin, and Braga, op. cit.

[83] 19 U.S.C. § 2463(b)(1).

[84] 19 U.S.C. § 2463(c).

[85] Provisions for the GSP Annual Review are set out at 15 C.F.R. § 2007.2(c)-(h).

[86] See the Office of Textiles and Apparel (OTEXA) website at http://otexa.ita.doc.gov/.

[87] United States Government Accountability Office, *International Trade: U.S. Trade Preference Programs Provide Important Benefits, but a More Integrated Approach would Better*

Ensure Programs Meet Shared Goals, GAO-08-443, March 2008, p. 11, http://www.gao.gov.

[88] The WTO Agreement on Textiles and Clothing (1995 to January 1, 2005) established a 10-year plan for multilaterally eliminating quotas on international trade in textiles and apparel products. It replaced the Multifibre Arrangement signed in 1974, as part of the General Agreement on Tariffs and Trade.

[89] United States Government Accountability Office, *International Trade: U.S. Trade Preference Programs Provide Important Benefits, but a More Integrated Approach Would Better Ensure Programs Meet Shared Goals*, GAO-08-443, March 2008, p. 12, http://www.gao.gov.

[90] Ibid.

[91] U.S. International Trade Commission, *Andean Trade Preference Act: Impact on U.S. Industries and Consumers and on Drug Crop Eradication and Crop Substitution, 2008*, Investigation No. 332-352, September 2008, pp. 3-11, http://www.usitc.gov.

[92] Congressional Budget Office, *Cost Estimate on H.R. 4284, An Act to Extend the Generalized System of Preferences and the Andean Trade Preference Act, and for Other Purposes*. Since the law also extended some customs user fees and increased the portion of large corporate (firms with income of more than $1 billion) estimated income tax payments due in July 2014, CBO estimated that the net impact of the legislation would actually be much lower.

[93] CRS estimates based on U.S. International Trade Commission figures. See also CRS Report RL33577, *U.S. International Trade: Trends and Forecasts*, by Dick K. Nanto and J. Michael Donnelly.

[94] Bernard Hoekman, William J. Martin, and Carlos A. Primo Braga, *Preference Erosion: The Terms of the Debate*, World Bank, May 2006.

[95] See Government Accountability Office, *U.S. Trade Preference Programs: An Overview of Use by Beneficiaries and U.S. Administrative Reviews*, GAO-07-1209, September 2007, p. 4.

[96] Martin Vaughan, "Grassley Throws Up Obstacle to Trade Preference Renewal," *Congress Daily*, September 8, 2006.

[97] U.S. Congress, House Committee on Ways and Means, *Hearing on the Operation, Impact, and Future of the U.S. Preference Programs,* 111th Congress, 1st sess., November 17, 2009. Testimony of William Reinsch, President, National Foreign Trade Council (NFTC). See also Testimony of David Love, Senior Vice President and Chief Supply Chain Officer, Levi Strauss & Co., San Francisco, California.

[98] Joseph J. Schatz, "Lawmakers Look to Trade Preferences to Boost Haiti's Recovery," *CQ Today*, March 10, 2010, p. 6.

[99] U.S. Congress, Senate Committee on Finance, *U.S. Preference Programs: Options for Reform*, 111th Cong., 2nd sess., March 9, 2010.

[100] U.S. Congress, House Committee on Ways and Means, *Hearing on the Operation, Impact, and Future of the U.S. Preference Programs,* 111th Cong., 1st sess., Testimony of Loren Yager, Director, International Affairs and Trade, GAO.

[101] 19 U.S.C. § 3706; Executive Office of the President, Proclamation 7350 of October 2, 2000, "To Implement the African Growth and Opportunity Act and to Designate Eritrea as a Beneficiary Developing Country for Purposes of the Generalized System of Preferences," 65 *Federal Register* 59321, October 4, 2000. Currently, 40 countries are eligible to receive AGOA preferences.

[102] CRS Report RL34702, *Potential Trade Effects of Adding Vietnam to the Generalized System of Preferences Program*, by Michael F. Martin and Vivian C. Jones.

[103] Center for Global Development, *Open Markets for the Poorest Countries*, p. 6; Paul Collier, *The Bottom Billion*, pp. 167-168, and Amy Tsul, "Senate Finance Chairman Baucus, Grassley Describe Trade Preference Reform Elements," *International Trade Daily*, March 10, 2010.

[104] U.S. Congress, Senate Committee on Finance, *U.S. Preference Programs: Options for Reform*, 111th Cong., 2nd sess., March 9, 2010, Statement of Senator Charles Grassley.

[105] 19 U.S.C. § 2462(e). The World Bank currently uses gross national income (GNI) per capita as its main indicator for classifying economies, and countries are determined to be "high income" if they have reached a per capita income level of $11,906 or more. See World Bank, *Country Classifications*, http://data.worldbank.org/about/country-classifications.

[106] The President already has authority to do this as outlined in GSP discretionary criteria. See 19 U.S.C.§ 2462(c)(2).

[107] House of Representatives, Office of Representative Jim McDermott, "Rep. McDermott Introduces Bill to Improve Trade Benefits to Poor Countries," Press Release, November 20, 2009.

[108] Third-country fabric provisions allow an apparel product to contain some fabric inputs originating anywhere in the world and still be imported duty-free under a preference program. The AGOA preference includes a Special Rule (in force until September 30, 2012) for lesser-developed beneficiaries allowing them to include a limited amount of third-party fabric in AGOA apparel imports.

[109] H.R. 4101 defines a "significant apparel supplier" as an LDC beneficiary from which total U.S. apparel imports in a calendar year exceed 2% of the aggregate square meter equivalents of all U.S. apparel imports in that year.

[110] U.S. Congress, House Committee on Ways and Means, *Hearing on the Operation, Impact, and Future of the U.S. Preference Programs*, 111th Cong., 1st sess., November 17, 2009, Statement for the Record, U.S. Preference Reform Working Group.

[111] Kimberley Ann Elliott, et al., *Open Markets for the Poorest Countries: Trade Preferences that Work.*, Center for Global Development, April 2010, p. 13.

[112] European Commission, *Generalized System of Preferences*, http://ec.europa.eu/trade/wider-agenda/development/generalised-system-of-preferences/index_en.htm.

[113] See Kimberly Ann Elliott, et al., *Open Markets for the Poorest Countries: Trade Preferences that Work*, Center for Global Development, April 2010.

[114] World Trade Organization, Ministerial Declaration, Annex F, December 18, 2005, WT/MIN(05)/DEC.

[115] For example, see U.S. Congress, House Committee on Ways and Means, *Hearing on the Operation, Impact, and Future of the U.S. Preference Programs*, 111th Cong., 1st sess., November 17, 2009, Statement for the Record, African Cotton and Textiles Industries Federation.

[116] United Nations Conference on Trade and Development (UNCTAD), *GSP - Handbook on the Scheme of Australia*, UNCTAD/ITCD/TSB/Misc.56, 2000.

[117] Kimberly Ann Elliott, et al., *Open Markets for the Poorest Countries: Trade Preferences that Work*, Center for Global Development, April 2010, pp. 9-10.

In: U.S. Trade Preferences...
Editor: Jonathan R. Ferreira
ISBN: 978-1-61324-378-7

Chapter 2

TRADE PREFERENCES FOR DEVELOPING COUNTRIES AND THE WORLD TRADE ORGANIZATION (WTO)*

Jeanne J. Grimmett

SUMMARY

Article I:1 of the General Agreement on Tariffs and Trade 1994 (GATT 1994) requires World Trade Organization (WTO) Members to grant most-favored-nation (MFN) treatment "immediately and unconditionally" to the like products of other Members with respect to tariffs and other trade-related measures. Programs such as the Generalized System of Preferences (GSP), under which developed countries grant preferential tariff rates to developing country goods, are facially inconsistent with this obligation because they accord goods of some countries more favorable tariff treatment than that accorded to like goods of other WTO Members. Because such programs have been viewed as trade-expanding, however, parties to the GATT provided a legal basis for one-way tariff preferences in a 1979 decision known as the Enabling Clause. The Enabling Clause was formally incorporated into the GATT 1994 upon the entry into force of the GATT Uruguay Round agreements on January 1, 1995. In 2004, the WTO Appellate Body ruled

* This is an edited, reformatted and augmented version of a Congressional Research Services publication, CRS Report for Congress RS22183, from www.crs.gov, dated January 21, 2011.

that the Clause allows developed countries to offer differing treatment to developing countries in a GSP program, but only if identical treatment is available to all similarly situated beneficiaries.

In addition to GSP programs, some WTO Members may also grant preferences to products of particular groups of countries that are more generous than GSP benefits. In such cases, Members have generally obtained time-limited WTO waivers of GATT Article I:l and, if needed, other GATT obligations. The United States holds temporary WTO waivers for tariff preferences granted to the former Trust Territory of the Pacific Islands and for three regional preference schemes:

(1) the Caribbean Basin Economic Recovery Act (CBERA), as amended; (2) the Andean Trade Preference Act (ATPA), as amended, and (3) the African Growth and Opportunity Act (AGOA). Congress has made the CBERA program permanent and has authorized through September 30, 2020, the expanded tariff benefits contained in the Caribbean Basin Trade Partnership Act and subsequent legislation particular to Haiti. The AGOA program is authorized through September 30, 2015. While the U.S. GSP program expired on December 31, 2010, Congress extended the Andean preference program through February 12, 2011.

In the 111th Congress, H.R. 1318 (Van Hollen) would have extended duty-free treatment for certain textile and apparel products and other goods from designated Reconstruction Opportunity Zones (ROZs) in Afghanistan and Pakistan until September 30, 2024, conditioning continued benefits on governmental compliance with various labor requirements. S. 496 (Cantwell) would have authorized the same through September 30, 2023, without added labor conditions. The House legislation was added to H.R. 1886, the Pakistan Enduring Assistance and Cooperation Enhancement Act of 2009, which passed the House June 11, 2009. H.R. 1886 was later appended to H.R. 2410, the Foreign Relations Authorization Act, FYs 2010 and 2011, which passed the House June 10, 2009. Assistance to Pakistan was later enacted into law without ROZ provisions.

Other 111th Congress trade preference legislation included H.R. 1837 (Engel) and S. 780 (Bill Nelson), which would have made Paraguay eligible for the ATPA program; H.R. 2702 (C. Smith), which would have limited GSP benefits for Brazil; H.R. 3039 (McDermott), which would have provided preferential tariff treatment to certain apparel from the Philippines; H.R. 4101 (McDermott), which would have expanded preferential trade benefits for least-developed countries (LDCs) and authorized the GSP program through December 31, 2019; S. 1141 (Feinstein), which would have granted duty-free treatment to textiles and apparel from 14 LDCs; and S. 1665 (Lugar), which would have made Paraguay and Uruguay eligible for ATPA benefits, expanded certain textile-related benefits under the program, and extended the program through December 31, 2012. No action was taken on any of these bills.

TRADE PREFERENCES AND GATT MFN REQUIREMENTS

As parties to the General Agreement on Tariffs and Trade 1994 (GATT 1994), World Trade Organization (WTO) Members must under Article I:1 of the GATT grant most-favored-nation (MFN) treatment[1] "immediately and unconditionally" to the like products of other Members with respect to customs duties and import charges, internal taxes and regulations, and other trade-related matters.[2] Thus, whenever a WTO Member accords a benefit or advantage to a product of one country, whether it is a WTO Member or not, the Member must accord the same benefit or advantage to the like product of all other WTO Members. Tariff preference programs for developing countries are facially inconsistent with this obligation as the favorable treatment provided by the granting country to the goods of a specific group of countries is not extended to all WTO Members. Because preference programs have been viewed as vehicles of trade liberalization and economic development for developing countries, however, GATT Parties have accommodated them in a series of joint actions.

In 1965, the GATT Parties added Part IV (Arts. XXXVI-XXXVIII) to the General Agreement, an amendment that recognizes the special economic needs of developing countries and asserts the principle of nonreciprocity. Under this principle, developed countries forego the receipt of reciprocal benefits for their negotiated commitments to reduce or eliminate tariffs and restrictions on the trade of less developed contracting parties.[3] Because of the underlying MFN issue, GATT Parties in 1971 adopted a waiver of Article I for the Generalized System of Preferences (GSP), which allowed developed contracting parties to accord more favorable tariff treatment to the products of developing countries for 10 years.[4] The waiver describes the GSP as a "system of generalized, nonreciprocal and nondiscriminatory preferences beneficial to the developing countries."

At the end of the GATT Tokyo Round in 1979, developing countries secured adoption of the Enabling Clause, a permanent deviation from MFN by joint decision of the GATT Contracting Parties. The Clause states that notwithstanding GATT Article I, "contracting parties may accord differential and more favourable treatment to developing countries, without according such treatment to other contracting parties" and applies this exception to: (1)

preferential tariff treatment in accordance with the GSP; (2) multilateral nontariff preferences negotiated under GATT auspices; (3) multilateral arrangements among less developed countries; and (4) special treatment of the least-developed countries" in the context of any general or specific measures in favour of developing countries."[5] The Enabling Clause has since been incorporated into the GATT 1994.[6]

In 1999, the WTO General Council adopted a decision, captioned "Preferential Tariff Treatment for Least-Developed Countries," which waived GATT Article I:1 until June 30, 2009, "to the extent necessary to allow developing country Members to provide preferential tariff treatment to products of least-developed countries (LDCs), designated as such by the United Nations, without being required to extend the same tariff rates to like products of any other Member."[7] Along with setting out various standards and notification and procedural requirements, the waiver, at paragraph 6, provides that it "does not affect in any way and is without prejudice to rights of Members in their actions pursuant to" the Enabling Clause. The waiver was recently extended until June 30, 2019.[8]

WTO Waivers for Certain Tariff Preferences

WTO Members maintaining preference programs or preferential trade agreements that fall outside the scope of the Enabling Clause or particular GATT articles may seek waivers of Article I:1 and other GATT obligations under Article IX:3 of the Agreement Establishing the World Trade Organization (WTO Agreement). Article IX:3 permits WTO Members as a whole to waive obligations imposed on a WTO Member by WTO multilateral agreements, including the GATT. A request for a GATT waiver must first be submitted by the requesting Member to the WTO Council for Trade in Goods, which, after considering the request, reports to the WTO General Council. The waiver becomes effective after the General Council agrees to the proposal.[9]

Preferential Trade Agreements

The European Union (EU) had argued that it could further deviate from Article I:1 MFN requirements for nonreciprocal free trade with developing countries under GATT Part IV, as well as Article XXIV, which provides an MFN exception for customs unions and free trade areas meeting specified conditions.[10] At issue was the Lomé IV Convention, a preferential, nonreciprocal trade arrangement between the European Economic Community (EEC) and African, Caribbean and Pacific (ACP) countries. The Convention extended beneficial tariff and quota treatment to ACP imports as well as development assistance to ACP countries. GATT panels concluded in unadopted 1993 and 1994 reports that such a deviation was not justified under either provision.[11] Regarding the Article XXIV claim, the 1994 report concluded that because Lomé IV involved non-GATT Parties, the Article did not cover the agreement and thus could not be used to justify the inconsistency with Article I of trade preferences for bananas imported from ACP countries.[12]

The European Union subsequently obtained a temporary waiver of GATT Article I:1 for the Lomé agreement; a waiver was later granted for the successor ACP-EC Partnership Agreement (Cotonou Agreement) until December 31, 2007.[13] The European Union has since been negotiating Economic Partnership Agreements (EPAs) with ACP countries to replace the Cotonou Agreement. Various WTO Members have raised concerns as to whether MFN clauses in the EPAs, under which trade benefits negotiated by ACP countries with third countries would be accorded to the European Union, are consistent with the Enabling Clause.[14]

Waivers for U.S. Preference Programs

Along with maintaining its long-standing GSP program,[15] the United States administers various regional preferences for which it holds WTO waivers. GATT Article I:1 has been waived for tariff preferences for the former Trust Territory of the Pacific Islands until December 31, 2016.[16] The United States has also obtained waivers for the following programs: (1) the Caribbean Basin Economic Recovery Act (CBERA), as amended,[17] through December 31, 2014; (2) the Andean Trade Preference Act (ATPA), as amended,[18] through December 31, 2014; and (3) the African Growth and Opportunity Act (AGOA),[19] through September 30, 2015.[20] These programs extend duty-free treatment that in some cases is subject to quantitative restrictions, and, thus, the WTO has agreed to waive not only GATT Article I:1 but also GATT Article XIII, paras. 1 and 2, which require nondiscrimination in administering quotas.

The United States submitted a waiver request for AGOA, as well as requests for renewals of expired or expiring waivers for the CBERA and ATPA programs, in February 2005.[21] Revised requests were submitted in

March 2009, reflecting legislative amendments to the CBERA and ATPA programs.[22] During this period, Brazil, China, India, and Pakistan raised questions on the U.S schemes focused primarily on textile issues, while Paraguay questioned why it had not been included in the ATPA program.[23] The U.S. requests were ultimately approved by the WTO Council on Trade in Goods in March 2009,[24] and by the WTO General Council in May 2009.[25]

Congress has made the CBERA program permanent and has authorized the expanded benefits contained in the Caribbean Basin Trade Partnership Act and later legislation particular to Haiti through September 30, 2020. The AGOA program is authorized through September 30, 2015. While the U.S. GSP program expired on December 31, 2010, Congress extended the Andean trade preference program as it applies to Colombia and Ecuador through February 12, 2011.[26]

WTO-Legality of Non-Trade Conditions in Preference Programs

In *European Communities—Conditions for the Granting of Tariff Preferences to Developing Countries,* the WTO Appellate Body (AB) explained how developed country WTO members may design preferential-tariff programs within the requirements of the Enabling Clause.[27] The dispute between India and the European Union (EU) stemmed from an EU Regulation which awarded tariff preferences to a closed group of 12 beneficiary countries on the condition that they combat illicit drug production (the Drug Arrangements). India brought the claim alleging that the Drug Arrangements were inconsistent with GATT Article I:1 and unjustified by the Enabling Clause.

The initial dispute panel, in a report issued on December 1, 2003, concluded that the EU was in violation of its WTO obligations, with one panelist dissenting on procedural grounds.[28] Addressing the nature of the Enabling Clause and its procedural implications, a two member majority first concluded that the Enabling Clause functions as an exception to the GATT Article I:1 MFN obligation and that, consequently, the burden of proof rests on the party that invokes the Enabling Clause as a defense. The lone dissenter argued that the MFN obligation does not apply to the Enabling Clause and that India did not properly bring the claim under the Clause. Employing a broad reading of the term "non-discriminatory" in the Clause's description of the

GSP, the panel concluded that developed countries were required to provide "identical tariff preferences" under GSP schemes to "all developing countries without differentiation, except for the implementation of a priori limitations."[29] Applying this standard, the panel then ruled that the Drug Arrangements were inconsistent with GATT Article I:1 and could not be justified under the Clause. The European Union appealed.

The Appellate Body report, issued on April 7, 2004, first addressed the relationship between GATT Article I:1 and the Enabling Clause. The AB upheld the panel's findings that the Enabling Clause is an exception to GATT Article I:1 and that the Clause does not exclude the applicability of Article I:1. The AB explained that the Enabling Clause is to be read together with Article I:1 in the procedural sense, since a challenged measure, such as the Drug Arrangements, is "submitted successively to the test of compatibility with the two provisions."[30] In other words, when the Enabling Clause is implicated, the dispute panel first examines whether a measure is consistent with Article I:1, "as the general rule," and, if it is found not to be so, the panel then examines whether the measure may be justified under the Clause.[31]

Noting the "vital role" played by the Enabling Clause "in promoting trade as a means of stimulating economic growth and development"[32] and the intent of WTO Members through the Clause to encourage the adoption of preference schemes, [33] the AB found that the Clause was not a typical GATT exception or defense. Thus, the AB modified the panel's finding and held that, unlike the ordinary practice with respect to GATT exceptions, under which exceptions are invoked only by the responding party, "it was incumbent upon [complainant] India to *raise* the Enabling Clause in making its claim of inconsistency with Article I:1 of the GATT 1994"[34] and to identify specific provisions of the Clause which it believed were violated by the respondent's measure.[35] At the same time, the burden of justifying GSP schemes under the cited Enabling Clause provisions still rests on a respondent. In application, the AB found that India sufficiently raised the issue, thereby placing the burden on the EU to justify the Drug Arrangements under the Clause.

Most importantly, the AB reversed the panel's substantive decision regarding the breadth of acceptable preference programs under the Enabling Clause. The AB found instead that developed countries can grant preferences beyond those provided in their GSP to developing countries with particular needs, but only if identical treatment is available to all similarly situated GSP beneficiaries. The AB elaborated that similarly situated GSP beneficiaries are all GSP beneficiaries that have the "'development, financial and trade needs' to which the treatment in question is intended to respond."[36] In reaching this conclusion, the AB reversed the panel's reading of the term "non-discriminatory" as used to define the GSP in the Enabling Clause. Even under the more expansive view of the Clause, however, the AB upheld the Panel's ruling that the EU had failed to prove that the Drug Arrangements were in fact "non-discriminatory." Two factors led the AB to its conclusion: (1) the closed list of beneficiary countries in the Drug Arrangements could not ensure that the preferences would be available to all GSP beneficiaries suffering from illicit drug production and trafficking, and (2) the Drug Arrangements did not set out objective criteria that distinguished beneficiaries under the Arrangements from other GSP beneficiaries.[37]

Before the WTO Dispute Settlement Body adopted the ruling, the U.S. representative stated, according to meeting minutes, that the United States was pleased that the Appellate Body had "reversed the Panel's finding that the Enabling Clause required developed countries under their GSP programs to provide *identical* preferences to *all* developing countries" and that the AB's decision "would help maintain the viability of GSP programs."[38] The United States raised concerns, however, about the AB's finding that complainant India needed to raise the Clause, but that the EU bore the burden of proving that the Drug Arrangements were consistent with the Clause. The United States questioned the legal basis for this "hybrid approach" suggesting that difficulties might ensue in allowing the complaining party to set the burden of proof for the respondent.

111TH CONGRESS LEGISLATION

In December 2009, Congress extended the GSP and Andean trade preference programs to December 31, 2010, continuing an existing denial of benefits to Bolivia.[39] While Congress has not renewed the GSP program, it enacted legislation in December 2010 extending Andean trade preferences, as accorded to Colombia and Ecuador, through February 12, 2011.[40] Andean benefits for Peru, which has been a party to a free trade agreement with the United States since February 2009, were terminated as of December 31, 2010, in the same enactment.[41] Earlier in the year, Congress authorized the extension of tariff benefits contained in the Caribbean Basin Trade Partnership Act and subsequent legislation particular to Haiti through September 30, 2020.[42]

Among other 111th Congress legislation, H.R. 1318 (Van Hollen) would have extended duty-free treatment for certain textile and apparel products and other goods from designated Reconstruction Opportunity Zones (ROZs) in

Afghanistan and Pakistan until September 30, 2024, and conditioned the continued eligibility of products from a designated ROZ for duty-free benefits on compliance by Pakistan or Afghanistan, as the case may be, with various labor-related requirements. S. 496 (Cantwell) would have also authorized such benefits for designated ROZs, but without added labor conditions, through September 30, 2023. The House legislation was added to H.R. 1886, the Pakistan Enduring Assistance and Cooperation Enhancement Act of 2009, which passed the House June 11, 2009. H.R. 1886 was subsequently appended to H.R. 2410, the Foreign Relations Authorization Act, Fiscal Years 2010-2011, which had passed the House June 10, 2009 (see Division B, Title IV), and was referred to and remained in the Senate Foreign Relations Committee.[43] In October 2009, assistance to Pakistan was authorized without the trade-related provisions contained in H.R. 1886.

Other 111th Congress trade preference bills included H.R. 1837 (Engel) and S. 780 (Bill Nelson), each of which would have made Paraguay eligible for the Andean preference program (see also S. 1665, below); H.R. 2702 (C. Smith), which would have required the President to suspend GSP benefits for Brazil within 30 days of enactment, subject to a national interest waiver, and permitted the President to reinstate benefits if he made certain certifications to congressional committees regarding Brazilian compliance with the Hague Convention on the Civil Aspects of International Child Abduction; H.R. 3039 (McDermott), which would have provided preferential tariff treatment to certain apparel items from the Philippines; H.R. 4101 (McDermott), which would have expanded preferential trade benefits for least-developed countries and extended the GSP program through December 31, 2019; S. 1141 (Feinstein), which would have granted duty-free treatment to textiles and apparel from 14 least-developed countries; and S. 1665 (Lugar), which would have made Paraguay and Uruguay eligible for the Andean preference program, expanded certain textile-related benefits under the program, and extended the program, as it related to Colombia, Peru, and, as added in the bill, Paraguay and Uruguay, through December 31, 2012.

End Notes

[1] While the WTO uses the term "most-favored-nation" to describe nondiscriminatory trade treatment, U.S. law has since 1998 referred to this treatment as "normal trade relations" (NTR) status. *See* P.L. 105-206, § 5003. This report uses the WTO terminology.

[2] The obligation to extend a benefit or advantage "unconditionally" to the goods of WTO Members aims to prevent Members from discriminating on the basis of origin and does

necessarily preclude them from conditioning the benefit or advantage itself. One WTO panel has stated that the obligation in GATT Article I:1 "to accord 'unconditionally' to third countries which are WTO Members an advantage which has been granted to any other country means that the extension of that advantage may not be made subject to conditions *with respect to the situation or conduct of those countries*." Panel Report, *Canada—Certain Measures Affecting the Automotive Industry*, para. 10.23,WT/DS139/R, WT/DS142/R (Feb. 11, 2000)(emphasis added)(panel interpretation not appealed). The panel continued: "An advantage can be granted subject to conditions without necessarily implying that it is not accorded 'unconditionally' to the like products of other Members. More specifically, the fact that conditions attached to such an advantage are not related to the imported product itself does not necessarily imply that such conditions are discriminatory with respect to the *origin* of imported products." *Id.* para. 10.24 (emphasis added).

[3] Edmond McGovern, INTERNATIONAL TRADE REGULATION § 9.212 (updated 1999)[hereinafter McGovern]. For discussion of how Part IV has been interpreted and applied, see WTO, GUIDE TO GATT LAW AND PRACTICE 1039-70 (6th ed. 1995).

[4] GATT, Generalized System of Preferences; Decision of 25 June 1971, L/3545 (June 28, 1971).

[5] GATT, Differential and More Favourable Treatment, Reciprocity and Fuller Participation of Developing Countries; Decision of 28 November 1979, L/4903 (Dec. 3, 1979). To describe the GSP, the Clause refers to the above-quoted language in the 1971 waiver.

[6] Agreement Establishing the World Trade Organization, Annex 1A, General Agreement on Tariffs and Trade 1994, para. 1(b)(iv); see Appellate Body Report, *European Communities—Conditions for the Granting of Tariff Preferences to Developing Countries*, para. 90.3, WT/DS246/AB/R (Apr. 7, 2004).

[7] Preferential Tariff Treatment for Least-Developed Countries; Decision on Waiver, WT/L/304 (June 17, 1999) (adopted June 15, 1999), at http://docsonline.wto.org/DDFDocuments/t/WT/L/304.DOC see also discussion in WTO Committee on Trade and Development, *Note on the Meeting of 2 March 1999*, at 2-6, WT/COMTD/M/24 (Apr. 27, 1999).

[8] Preferential Tariff Treatment for Least-Developed Countries; Decision on Extension of Waiver, WT/L/759 (May 29, 2009)(adopted May 27, 2009).

[9] Article IX:3 of the WTO Agreement provides that a decision on a waiver of a GATT obligation requires a three-fourths vote of the WTO Members. Under a decision adopted by the WTO General Council in 1995, Members will resort to a vote only if a decision cannot first be reached by consensus (i.e., without objection). This procedure does not preclude a Member, however, from asking for a vote at the time the decision is taken. WTO, Decision-Making Procedures under Articles IX and XII of the WTO Agreement, WT/L/93 (Nov. 24, 1993). Consensus decision-making is the norm in GATT practice. See WTO Agreement, Art. IX:1.

[10] As of December 1, 2009, "European Union" replaced "European Communities" as the official name of this WTO Member. The change comes as a result of the entry into force of the Treaty of Lisbon, under which the European Union replaced and succeeded the European Community. See Verbal Note from the Council of the European Union and the Commission of the European Communities, WT/L/779 (Nov. 30, 2009). The terms European Communities and EC still appear in older WTO materials, including panel and Appellate Body reports, bilateral procedural agreements in particular disputes, and communications to the WTO Dispute Settlement Body. Except for references to any such older WTO documents or other governmental materials using this name, this report uses "European Union" or the acronym "EU" in the report text or notes regardless of the time period being discussed. For further information, see *European Union or Communities?*, at

http://www.wto.org/english/thewto_e/countries_e/european_union_or_communities_popup.htm.

[11] McGovern, *supra* note 3, § 9.212.

[12] Panel Report, *EEC—Import Regime for Bananas*, paras. 156-164, DS38/R (1994), *as reprinted in* 34 INT'L LEGAL MATERIALS 180 (1995).

[13] GATT, L/7604 (Dec. 19, 1994); WTO, WT/L/436 (Dec. 7, 2001).

[14] See minutes of the WTO General Council, including May 7, 2008, at 21-27, WT/GC/M/114, and February 5-6, 2008, at 23-28, WT/GC/M/113. See also WTO Trade Policy Review Body, *Trade Policy Review, European Communities;Record of the Meeting*, para. 189, WT/TPRM/M/214 (June 8, 2009)(statement by Chile).

[15] The U.S. GSP program was enacted in the Trade Act of 1974, P.L. 93-618, Title V, as amended, 19 U.S.C. §§ 2461-2467. For further discussion of the program, see CRS Report RL33663, *Generalized System of Preferences: Background and Renewal Debate*, by Vivian C. Jones.

[16] WTO, United States—Former Trust Territory of the Pacific Islands; Decision of 27 July 2007, WT/L/694 (Aug. 1, 2007)(covers Republic of the Marshall Islands, Federated States of Micronesia, Commonwealth of the Northern Mariana Islands, and Republic of Palau).

[17] Caribbean Basin Economic Recovery Act (CBERA), P.L. 98-67, as amended, 19 U.S.C. §§ 2701-2706. For further information, see CRS Report RL33951, *U.S. Trade Policy and the Caribbean: From Trade Preferences to Free Trade Agreements*, by J. F. Hornbeck.

[18] Andean Trade Preference Act (ATPA), P.L. 102-182, as amended, 19 U.S.C. §§ 3201-3206. The WTO waiver covers amendments made to the ATPA program by the Andean Trade Promotion and Drug Eradication Act, P.L. 107-210, §§ 3101-3108. Bolivia, Colombia, Ecuador, and Peru are authorized to be designated as beneficiary countries under the ATPA; the President suspended Bolivia's designation as a beneficiary country, however, effective December 15, 2008. See *infra* notes 36-37 and accompanying text. For further discussion of the Andean program, see CRS Report RS22548, *ATPA Renewal: Background and Issues*, by M. Angeles Villarreal.

[19] African Growth and Opportunity Act (AGOA), P.L. 106-200, Title I, as amended, 19 U.S.C. §§ 2466a-2466b, 3701- 3722 AGOA preferences are available to sub-Saharan African countries. See generally CRS Report RL31772, *U.S. Trade and Investment Relationship with Sub-Saharan Africa: The African Growth and Opportunity Act* , by Vivian C. Jones.

[20] See WTO documents WT/L/753 (CBERA), WT/L/754 (AGOA), and WT/L/755 (ATPA).

[21] See WTO documents G/C/W/508 (CBREA); G/C/W/509 (AGOA); and G/C/W/510 and G/C/W/510/Add.1 (ATPA).

[22] The March 2009 requests are contained in the following WTO documents: G/C/W/508/Rev.2 (CBERA); G/C/W/509/Rev.2 (AGOA); and G/C/W/510/Rev.2 (ATPA). The CBERA request cites changes to the Caribbean program enacted under the United States-Caribbean Trade Partnership Act (P.L. 106-200, Title II, as amended), as well as the Haitian Hemispheric Opportunity through Partnership Encouragement Act of 2006, as amended by the Haitian Hemispheric Opportunity through Partnership Encouragement Act of 2008 (P.L. 110-246, Title IV).

[23] Paraguay had blocked the U.S. requests, suggesting compensation as a means of alleviating alleged trade damage caused by its exclusion from the Andean program. See minutes of the WTO Council on Trade in Goods, including July 1, 2008, at 1-2, G/C/M/94; May 22, 2008, at 2-4, G/C/M/93; March 11, 2008, at 2-3, G/C/M/92; November 23, 2007, at 3-4, G/C/M/91; May 21, 2007, at 3-5, G/C/M/89; November 20, 2006, at 15-21, G/C/M/86; July

12, 2006, at 3-8, G/C/M/85; May 9, 2006, at 3-11, G/C/M/84; March 10, 2006, at 3-13, G/C/M/83; and November 10, 2005, at 9-12, G/C/M/82.

[24] WTO News Item, Goods Council agrees on 2009 chairs, waivers for U.S. trade-preference programmes (Mar. 24, 2009), at http://www.wto.org/english/news_e/news09_e/good_24 mar09_e.htm. See also *Paraguay Agrees to Grant U.S. Waiver Request for AGOA, ATPDEA, CBERA*, INSIDE U.S. TRADE, Mar. 20, 2009, at 4. Legislation has been introduced in the 111th Congress to include Paraguay as an eligible country for purposes of the ATPA. See *infra* p. 8.

[25] WTO, General Council, Minutes of Meeting, May 26-27, 2009, at 50-54, WT/GC/M/120 (Aug. 21, 2009).

[26] See additional discussion of the status of current programs under "111th Congress Legislation," *infra* pp. 7-8.

[27] Appellate Body Report, *European Communities—Conditions for the Granting of Tariff Preferences to Developing Countries*, WT/DS246/AB/R (Apr. 7, 2004)[hereinafter EC Preferences AB Report].

[28] Panel Report, *European Communities—Conditions for the Granting of Tariff Preferences to Developing Countries*, WT/DS246/R (Dec. 1, 2003).

[29] *Id.* para. 7.161.

[30] EC Preferences AB Report, *supra* note 27, para. 102.

[31] *Id.* para. 101.

[32] *Id.* para. 106.

[33] *Id.* para. 114.

[34] *Id.* para. 125 (emphasis in original)

[35] *Id.* para. 115.

[36] *Id.* para. 173.

[37] *Id.* paras 187-188.

[38] Dispute Settlement Body, *Minutes of Meeting*, Apr. 20, 2004, paras. 58-59, WT/DSB/M/167 (May 27, 2004)(emphasis in original).

[39] P.L. 111-124, §§ 1, 2(a), amending Trade Act of 1974, P.L. 93-618, Title V, § 505, 19 U.S.C. § 2465, and Andean Trade Preference Act (ATPA), P.L. 102-182, Title II, § 208(a), 19 U.S.C.§ 3206(a).

[40] P.L. 111-344, § 201(a), (b), amending ATPA, P.L. 102-182, §§ 208(a)(1)(A),(2), 19 U.S.C. §§ 3206(a)(1)(A),(2). An October 2008 enactment, P.L. 110-436, had extended the GSP and Andean programs to December 31, 2009, with limitations on Andean benefits for both Ecuador and Bolivia. In amending § 208(a) of the ATPA, 19 U.S.C. § 3206(a), the 2008 law granted benefits to Ecuador until June 30, 2009, permitting them to continue through December 31, 2009, unless the President determined and reported to Congress that Ecuador *did not* satisfy certain statutory criteria. In addition, while benefits were also extended to Bolivia through June 30, 2009, the benefits were allowed to continue through December 31, 2009, only if the President determined and reported that Bolivia *did* satisfy these criteria. Two months after enactment, Bolivia was suspended as a beneficiary country under the ATPA and the Andean Trade Promotion and Drug Eradication Act of 2002, due to "the Bolivian government's failure to meet the programs' counternarcotics cooperation criteria." Andean Trade Preference Act (ATPA), as Amended: Notice Regarding Eligibility of Bolivia, 73 Fed. Reg. 57158 (Oct. 1, 2008); Proclamation No. 8323, para. 4, 73 Fed. Reg. 72677, 72679 (Nov. 28, 2008). In June 2009, the President made determinations that effectively maintained each country's existing status, thus permitting continued benefits for Ecuador and denying the extension of benefits to Bolivia. The 2009 statute continued this

denial of Andean trade benefits to Bolivia by extending the negative effect of the President's June 2009 determination to December 31, 2010. The December 2010 enactment has further extended this negative effect through February 12, 2011, while expressly extending ATPA benefits to Ecuador through the same date.

[41] P.L. 111-344, § 201(a), adding ATPA, P.L. 102-182, § 208(a)(1)(B), 19 U.S.C. §§ 3206(a)(1)(B). The United States has entered into free trade agreements (FTAs) with two ATPA beneficiaries, Colombia and Peru, the agreement with Peru having been approved in P.L. 110-138 and entered into force February 1, 2009. See U.S. Peru-Trade Promotion Agreement, at http://www.ustr.gov/trade. Legislation implementing the FTA with Colombia was introduced in the 110th Congress, 2d Sess. (H.R. 5724, S. 2830), but expedited legislative procedures that would have applied to the House bill were suspended by the House shortly thereafter (H.Res. 1092). Although it has been U.S. policy to remove a beneficiary country from tariff preference programs once it becomes an FTA party (see, e.g., Dominican Republic-Central America-United States Free Trade Agreement Implementation Act, P.L. 109-53, § 201(a)(2),(3) (removal from GSP; removal from CBERA, with limited exceptions); United States-Peru Trade Promotion Agreement Implementation Act, P.L. 110-138, § 201(a)(2)(removal from GSP)), Peru continued to be a beneficiary country under the Andean trade preference program until benefits were moved in December 2010. See Notice of Correction, 74 Fed. Reg. 7493 (Feb. 17, 2009).

[42] Haiti Economic Lift Program Act of 2010, P.L. 111-171, § 3.

[43] Enhanced Partnership with Pakistan Act of 2009, P.L. 111-73.

In: U.S. Trade Preferences…
Editor: Jonathan R. Ferreira

ISBN: 978-1-61324-378-7

Chapter 3

GENERALIZED SYSTEM OF PREFERENCES: BACKGROUND AND RENEWAL DEBATE*

Vivian C. Jones

SUMMARY

The U.S. Generalized System of Preferences (GSP) program provides non-reciprocal, duty-free tariff treatment to certain products imported from designated beneficiary developing countries (BDCs). The United States, the European Union, and other developed countries have implemented similar programs since the 1970s in order to promote economic growth in developing countries by stimulating their exports. The U.S. program was first authorized in Title V of the Trade Act of 1974, and was most recently extended until December 31, 2010, in P.L. 111-124 for all GSP beneficiary countries not covered by the African Growth and Opportunity Act (AGOA). Since GSP will expire at the end of 2010, this and other trade preference programs may continue to be a the focus of congressional attention in the 112th Congress.

The GSP is one of several trade preference programs that provide non-reciprocal, duty-free access to goods from developing and least-developed beneficiary countries. Other U.S. trade preference programs include the African Growth and Opportunity Act (AGOA), the Andean Trade Preference Act (ATPA), and the Caribbean Basin Initiative (CBI).

---

* This is an edited, reformatted and augmented version of a Congressional Research Services publication, CRS Report for Congress RL33663, from www.crs.gov, dated January 13, 2011.

In recent years, renewal of trade preferences programs in general, and of the GSP program in particular, has been somewhat controversial in Congress. Some Members have expressed the view that some of the more advanced BDCs, such as Brazil and India, continue to receive benefits even while they actively contribute to the impasse in multilateral World Trade Organization (WTO) Doha Development Agenda (DDA) talks. Some Members have also questioned whether more "advanced" developing countries should be receiving benefits under unilateral preference programs at all, and propose ending or limiting their benefits in favor of providing a greater share of benefits to least-developed countries (LDCs). Other Members have proposed granting duty-free, quota-free access (DFQF) to developing countries under the African Growth and Opportunity Act (who are also GSP beneficiaries), which could potentially also be extended to other GSP countries.

On December 15, 2010, the House approved H.R. 6517, the Omnibus Trade Act of 2010, which, in part, sought to extend the GSP program through June 30, 2012. On December 22, 2010, the Senate passed an amended version of H.R. 6517 that did not include GSP renewal. The amended version subsequently passed in the House on the same date (P.L. 111-344). Other GSP-related legislation in the 111th Congress included S. 1141 and H.R. 4101 which sought additional preferences for non-African LDCs. Other bills referring to GSP included H.R. 1969 and companion bill S. 1159, which sought to prohibit GSP authority for Vietnam.

This report presents, first, a brief history, economic rationale, and legal background leading to the establishment of the GSP. A brief comparison of GSP programs worldwide, especially as they compare to the U.S. system, is also presented. Second, the report presents a discussion of U.S. implementation of the GSP, along with the present debate surrounding its renewal and legislative developments to date. Third, an analysis of the U.S. program's effectiveness and the positions of various stakeholders is presented. Fourth, implications of the expiration of the U.S. program and possible options for Congress are discussed.

INTRODUCTION

The Generalized System of Preferences (GSP) program provides preferential tariff treatment to certain products imported from designated developing countries. The United States, the European Union, and other developed countries have implemented such programs since the 1970s in order to promote economic growth in developing countries by stimulating their exports.

The U.S. program (as established by Title V of the Trade Act of 1974) was last extended through December 31, 2010, in P.L. 111-124. A move to extend GSP until June 30, 2012 as part of the Omnibus Trade Act of 2010 (H.R. 6517, became P.L. 111-344) failed when the Senate passed an amendment in the nature of a substitute that did not contain the GSP provision, and the House subsequently passed the amended version. The African Growth and Opportunity Acceleration Act of 2004 (P.L. 108-274) previously extended GSP preferences for all beneficiary developing sub-Saharan African countries under the African Growth and Opportunity Act (AGOA) through September 30, 2015.[1] Therefore, even though the GSP program has lapsed, AGOA beneficiaries that are also eligible for GSP, will continue to receive GSP preferences.

In the 111th Congress, the House Ways and Means and Senate Finance Committees (the committees with primary jurisdiction) expressed interest in examining the effectiveness of the GSP and other trade preference programs, and both held hearings—Ways and Means in November 2009 and Senate Finance in March 2010—on the effectiveness of, and suggested modifications to, the GSP and other preference programs.

This report presents, first, a brief history, economic rationale, and legal framework behind establishment of the Generalized System of Preferences, and a brief comparison of GSP programs worldwide. Second, the report presents a description of U.S. implementation of the GSP program, along with recent legislative developments and the debate surrounding its renewal. Third, it provides a brief analysis of the U.S. program's effectiveness and the positions of various stakeholders. Fourth, the report analyzes implications of GSP expiration and options for Congress.

History and Rationale of the GSP

The basic principle behind the GSP is to provide certain goods originating in developing countries with preferential market access to developed-country markets in the form of lower tariff rates (or as in the U.S. case, duty-free status) in order to spur economic growth in the poorer countries. The program was first adopted internationally in 1968 by the United Nations Conference on Trade and Development (UNCTAD) at the UNCTAD II Conference.[2]

Economic Basis

The GSP was established based on an economic theory that preferential tariff rates in developed country markets could promote export-driven industry growth in developing countries. It was believed that this, in turn, would help to free beneficiaries from heavy dependence on trade in primary products, whose slow long-term growth and price instability contributed to chronic trade deficits.[3] It was thought that only the markets of industrialized trading partners were large enough to provide enough economic stimulus to attain these goals.[4]

Some economists also mention that the GSP was established, in part, as a means of reconciling two widely divergent economic perspectives of trade equity that arose during early negotiations on the General Agreement on Tariffs and Trade (GATT).[5] Industrialized, developed nations argued that the most-favored-nation principle[6] should be the fundamental principle governing multilateral trade, while less-developed countries believed that equal treatment of unequal trading partners did not constitute equity, and called for "special and differential treatment" for developing countries. GSP schemes thus became one of the means of offering a form of special treatment that developing nations sought while allaying the fears of developed countries that tariff "disarmament" might create serious disruptions in their domestic markets.[7]

Due to differences in developed countries' economic structures and tariff programs—as well as different domestic industries and products each wanted to shield from such competition—it proved difficult to create one unified system of identical tariff concessions. Therefore, the GSP became a system of individual national schemes based on common goals and principles—each with a view toward providing developing countries with generally equivalent opportunities for export growth.[8] As a result, the preference-granting countries implemented various individual schemes of *temporary, generalized, non-reciprocal, non-discriminatory* preferences under which tariffs were lowered or eliminated on certain imports from developing countries.

As a condition for providing such tariff preferences, GSP preference-granting countries reserved the right to (1) exclude certain countries; (2) determine product coverage; (3) determine rules of origin governing the preference; (4) determine the duration of the scheme; (5) reduce any preferential margins accruing to developing countries by continuing to lower or remove tariffs as a result of multilateral negotiations; (6) prevent the concentration of benefits among a few countries; (7) include safeguard mechanisms or "escape" clauses; and (8) place caps on the volume of duty-free trade entering under their programs.[9]

Although GSP programs were intended to be temporary, an international legal framework under the GATT (as discussed below) was developed to allow these programs to continue. Additionally, many developed countries have also decided to grant additional market access, through GSP or other preferential programs, to products of countries they designate as least-developed countries (LDCs). At the sixth World Trade Organization (WTO) Ministerial Conference in Hong Kong in December 2005, developed country WTO members and "developing country members declaring themselves in a position to do so" agreed to deepen this commitment by providing "duty-free and quota-free market [DFQF] access on a lasting basis, for all products originating from all least developed countries by 2008 or no later than the start of the implementation period in a manner that ensures stability, security and predictability."[10] Members "facing difficulties" with providing such access would be permitted to exempt 3% of all tariff lines, provided they take steps to achieve the goal of total duty-and quota-free access by incrementally building on the list of covered products.[11] Since DDA talks have been suspended, this duty-free/quota-free offer seems to be in jeopardy, at least on a multilateral basis.

International Legal Framework[12]

Because it is a preference program, by its very nature, the GSP posed a problem under the GATT in that the granting of preferences would be facially inconsistent with the fundamental obligation placed on GATT Parties in GATT Article I:1 to grant most-favored-nation (MFN) tariff treatment to the products of all other GATT Parties. As noted, however, preference programs were viewed as vehicles of trade liberalization and economic development for developing countries. Thus, GATT Parties accommodated them in a series of joint actions.

In 1965, the GATT Parties added Part IV to the General Agreement, an amendment that recognizes the special economic needs of developing countries and asserts the principle of non-reciprocity. Under this principle, developed countries forego the receipt of reciprocal benefits for their negotiated commitments to reduce or eliminate tariffs and restrictions on the trade of less developed contracting parties.[13] Because of the underlying MFN issue, GATT Parties in 1971 adopted a waiver of Article I for GSP programs, which allowed developed contracting parties to accord more favorable tariff treatment to the products of developing countries for 10 years.[14] The GSP was described in the decision as a "system of generalized, non-reciprocal and non-discriminatory preferences beneficial to the developing countries."

At the end of the Tokyo Round of Multilateral Trade Negotiations in 1979, developing countries secured adoption of the Enabling Clause, a permanent deviation from MFN by joint decision of the GATT Contracting Parties.[15] The Clause states that notwithstanding GATT Article I, "contracting parties may accord differential and more favorable treatment to developing countries, without according such treatment to other contracting parties" (¶1) and applies this exception to:

> a) Preferential tariff treatment accorded by developed contracting parties to products originating in developing countries in accordance with the Generalized System of Preferences;
> b) Differential and more favorable treatment with respect to the provisions of the General Agreement concerning non-tariff measures governed by the provisions of instruments multilaterally negotiated under the auspices of the GATT;
> c) Regional or global arrangements entered into amongst less-developed contracting parties for the mutual reductions or elimination of tariffs and, in accordance with criteria or conditions which may be prescribed by the CONTRACTING PARTIES for the mutual reduction or elimination of non-tariff measures, on products imported from one another;
> d) Special treatment on the least developed among the developing countries in the context of any general or specific measures in favour of developing countries (2).

To describe the GSP, the Clause refers to the above-quoted description in the 1971 waiver (i.e., a "system of generalized, non-reciprocal and non-discriminatory preferences beneficial to the developing countries").[16] Among other things, the Clause further provides, at 3(c), that any differential and more favorable treatment provided under the Clause "shall in the case of such treatment accorded by developed contracting parties to developing countries be designed and, if necessary, modified, to respond positively to the development, financial and trade needs of developing countries."

In addition, if a GATT Party (now WTO Member) who has instituted a GSP program subsequently takes action "to introduce modification or withdrawal of the differential treatment so provided," the Member is required to notify and consult with other WTO Members. Specifically, 4(a) requires the acting Member to notify WTO Members as a whole and to "furnish them with all the information they may deem appropriate relating to such action." Further, under 4(b), the Member must "afford adequate opportunity for prompt consultations at the request of any interested contracting party with respect to any difficulty or matter that may arise." If requested by any such interested party, WTO Members must as a whole consult with all WTO Members concerned over the issue at hand with the aim of reaching a solution that is satisfactory to all such Members. This requirement does not affect any Member's rights under the GATT.[17]

Paragraph 7 of the Clause provides that the less-developed WTO Members "expect that their capacity to make contributions or negotiated concessions or take other mutually agreed action under the provisions and procedures of the General Agreement would improve with their progressive development of their economies and improvement in their trade situation and they would accordingly expect to participate more fully in the framework of rights and obligations under the General Agreement." This paragraph is generally considered to support the "graduation" of a beneficiary country out of a grantor's GSP program by the grantor, either entirely or with respect to particular products, once the beneficiary country has attained a certain level of economic development.[18] The Enabling Clause does not contain express criteria or procedures for graduation, however, leaving grantor countries to establish criteria on a unilateral basis.

The Enabling Clause also states that it "would remain open for the CONTRACTING PARTIES to consider on an ad hoc basis under the GATT provisions for joint action any proposals for differential and more favorable treatment not falling within the scope of this paragraph," that is, a program that does not fit within one of the four categories described above.[19] This provision suggests the use of GATT waivers for more ambitious programs; in practice, waivers have been adopted for a variety of such programs, including several U.S. non-GSP tariff preferences.[20]

The Enabling Clause was incorporated into the GATT 1994 upon the entry into force of the Uruguay Round agreements on January 1, 1995.[21] In 1999, the WTO General Council adopted a decision, captioned "Preferential Tariff Treatment for Least-Developed Countries," which waived GATT Article I:1 until June 30, 2009, "to the extent necessary to allow developing country Members to provide preferential tariff treatment to products of least-developed countries (LDCs), designated as such by the United Nations, without being required to extend the same tariff rates to like products of any other Member."[22] Along with setting out various standards and notification and procedural requirements, the waiver, at paragraph 6, provides that it "does not affect in any way and is without prejudice to rights of Members in their actions pursuant to" the Enabling Clause. The waiver was recently extended until June 30, 2019.[23]

In addition, in a WTO dispute proceeding brought by India challenging special GSP benefits maintained by the European Communities (EC), *European Communities—Conditions for the Granting of Tariff Preferences to Developing Countries* (WT/DS246), the WTO Appellate Body addressed the issue of the extent to which a granting country may accord such benefits within a GSP program to countries meeting a separate set of criteria. The dispute stemmed from an EC Regulation which awarded tariff preferences to a closed group of 12 beneficiary countries on the condition that they combat illicit drug production (Drug Arrangements). India claimed that the Drug Arrangements were inconsistent with GATT Article I:1 and could not be justified by the Enabling Clause. In its 2004 report, the Appellate Body ruled that developed countries may grant preferences beyond those provided in their GSP to countries with particular needs, but only if identical treatment is available to all similarly situated GSP beneficiaries.[24] Among other things, the Appellate Body cited ¶ 3(c) of the Enabling Clause, providing that any differential and more favorable treatment provided under the Clause "shall ... be designed and, if necessary modified to respond positively to the development, financial and trade needs of developing countries."[25]

Comparison of International GSP Programs

One economist has referred to the Generalized System of Preferences as a non-homogeneous set of national schemes sharing certain common characteristics.[26] Generally, each preference-granting country extends to qualifying developing countries (as determined by each benefactor) an exemption from duties (reduced tariffs or duty-free access) on most manufactured products and certain "non-sensitive" agricultural products. Product coverage and the type of preferential treatment offered vary widely.[27]

Although most GSP schemes (including the U.S. program) admit eligible products duty-free, some countries provide tariff reductions, rather than complete exemption from duties.[28] The Australian system, for example, is based on a five percentage point margin of preference. When the Australian

General Tariff (GT) is 5% or higher, the amount of the tariff is reduced by 5% for products of beneficiary countries. When the GT rate is 5% or less, the preferential rate is zero.[29]

In the WTO, developing country status is generally based on self-determination. However, with regard to GSP, each preference-granting country establishes particular criteria and conditions for defining and identifying developing country beneficiaries. Consequently, the list of beneficiaries and exceptions may vary greatly between countries. If political or economic changes have taken place in a beneficiary country, it might be excluded from GSP programs in some countries (such as the United States) but not in others. Most countries, including the United States, also exclude countries if they have entered into another kind of commercial arrangement (e.g., a free trade agreement) with any other GSP-granting developed country.

In terms of additional GSP product coverage for LDCs, the European Community program, which offers duty-free access or reduced tariffs for "everything but arms,"[30] is currently perhaps the most inclusive. GSP-granting countries may also have incentive-based programs that provide enhanced benefits for beneficiary countries that meet certain additional criteria. For example, in 2007 the European Community implemented a regulation that grants additional GSP benefits to those countries that have demonstrated their commitment to sustainable development and internationally recognized worker rights.[31]

Each preference-granting nation also has safeguards in place to ensure that any significant increases in imports of a certain product do not adversely affect the receiving country's domestic market. Generally, these restrictions take the form of quantitative limits on goods entering under GSP. Under Japan's system, for example, imports of certain products under the preference are limited by quantity or value (whichever is applicable) on a first-come, first-served basis as administered on a monthly (or daily, as indicated) basis. For other products, import ceilings and maximum country amounts are set by prior allotment.[32] The United States quantitatively limits imports under the GSP program by placing "competitive need limit" (CNL) thresholds on the quantity or value of commodities entering duty-free, as discussed in more detail below.

Each GSP benefactor also has criteria for graduation—the point at which beneficiaries no longer qualify for benefits because they have reached a certain level of development. Most preference-granting countries require mandatory graduation based on a certain level of income per capita based on World Bank calculations. Some programs, such as the European Union's, also specifically provide for graduation of certain GSP recipients with respect to individual sectors of the economy.

U.S. Implementation

Congress first authorized the U.S. Generalized System of Preferences scheme in Title V of the Trade Act of 1974 (P.L. 93-618), as amended.[33] P.L. 93-618 authorizes the President to grant duty-free treatment under the GSP for any eligible product from any beneficiary developing country (BDC) or least-developed beneficiary developing country (LDBDC), provides the President with economic criteria in deciding whether to take any such action, and also specifies certain criteria for designating eligible countries and products.[34]

Based on the statutory requirements which countries must meet—and continue to practice—while participating in the program, the U.S. GSP program might be characterized as a foreign policy tool as well as an international trade program. Although GSP benefits are non-reciprocal, certain criteria speak to important U.S. commercial interests, such as ensuring "equitable and reasonable" access in the beneficiaries' market to U.S. products, protecting intellectual property rights, and preventing the seizure of property belonging to U.S. citizens or businesses. In addition, since certain "import sensitive" products are excluded from eligibility and quantitative/ value limitations apply to any eligible imports, the economic costs of the preference are quite small.

Beneficiary Countries

When designating BDCs and LDBDCs, the President is directed to take into account certain mandatory and discretionary criteria. The law prohibits (with certain exceptions) the President from extending GSP treatment to certain countries, as follows[35]:

- other industrial countries (Australia, Canada, European Union member states, Iceland, Japan, Monaco, New Zealand, Norway, and Switzerland are specifically excluded);
- communist countries, unless they are a WTO member, a member of the International Monetary Fund and receive Normal Trade Relations

(NTR) treatment; must also not be "dominated or controlled by international communism;"

- countries that collude with other countries to withhold supplies or resources from international trade or raise the price of goods in a way that could cause serious disruption to the world economy;
- countries that provide preferential treatment to the products of another developed country in a manner likely to have an significant adverse impact on U.S. commerce;
- countries that have nationalized or expropriated the property of U.S. citizens, or otherwise infringe on U.S. citizens' property rights, including patents, trademarks, or copyrights; countries that have taken steps to repudiate or nullify existing contracts or agreements of U.S. citizens (or corporations, partnerships, or associations that are 50% or more owned by U.S. citizens) in a way that would nationalize or seize ownership or control of the property; or countries that have imposed or enforced taxes or other restrictive conditions on measures on the property of U.S. citizens; *unless* the President determines that compensation is being made, good faith negotiations are in progress, or a dispute has been handed over to arbitration in the Convention for the Settlement of Investment Disputes or another forum;
- countries that have failed to act in good faith in recognizing as binding or in enforcing arbitral awards in favor of U.S. citizens (or corporations, partnerships, or associations that are 50% or more owned by U.S. citizens); and
- countries that grant sanctuary from prosecution to any individual or group that has committed an act of international terrorism, or has not taken steps to support U.S. efforts against terrorism.

Mandatory criteria also require that beneficiary countries:

- have taken or be taking steps to grant internationally recognized worker rights (including collective bargaining, freedom from compulsory labor, minimum age for employment of children, and acceptable working conditions with respect to minimum wages, hours of work, occupational safety and health); and
- implement their commitments to eliminate the worst forms of child labor.[36]

The President is also directed to consider certain discretionary criteria ("factors affecting country designation"), such as the following:

- the country's expressed desire to be designated a beneficiary developing country for purposes of the U.S. program;
- the level of economic development of the country;
- whether or not other developed countries are extending similar preferential tariff treatment to the country;
- its commitment to a liberal trade policy;
- the extent to which it provides adequate protection of intellectual property rights;
- the extent to which it has taken action to reduce trade-distorting investment policies and practices, and to reduce or eliminate barriers to trade in services; and
- whether or not it has taken steps to grant internationally recognized worker rights.[37]

The law further authorizes the President, based on the required and discretionary factors mentioned above, to withdraw, suspend or limit GSP treatment for any beneficiary developing country at any time.[38]

Reporting Requirements

The President must advise Congress of any changes in beneficiary developing country status, as necessary.[39] The President must also submit an annual report to Congress on the status of internationally recognized worker rights within each BDC, including findings of the Secretary of Labor with respect to the beneficiary country's implementation of its international commitments to eliminate the worst forms of child labor.[40]

Least-Developed Beneficiaries

The President is also authorized by statute to designate any BDC as a least-developed beneficiary (LDBDC), based on an assessment of the conditions and factors previously mentioned.[41] Although factors such as per capita income level, economic stability, and quality of life indicators (on which the United Nations-designated list of LDCs is based) are taken into account,[42] the U.S. administration also assesses the level of compliance with other GSP statutory requirements and comments from the public (as requested in the Federal Register) before identifying a country as "least-developed" for purposes of the GSP.[43]

Products

The Trade Act of 1974 authorizes the President to designate certain imports as eligible for duty-free treatment under the GSP after receiving advice from the ITC.[44] "Import sensitive" products specifically excluded from preferential treatment are most textiles and apparel goods; watches; footwear and other accessories; most electronics, steel, and glass products; and certain agricultural products subject to tariff-rate quotas.[45] The lists of eligible products and the list of beneficiary developing countries are reviewed and revised annually by the GSP Subcommittee.[46] Any modifications to these lists usually take effect on July 1 of the following calendar year.[47]

In terms of product coverage, more than 3,400 products are currently eligible for duty-free treatment, and about 1,400 additional articles originating in LDBDCs may receive similar treatment (see Table A-1). Leading imports in 2009 under the GSP program included petroleum products, especially crude oil; silver and gold necklaces; radial tires; and aluminum alloy plates, sheet, and strip.[48]

Competitive Need Limits

The law establishes "competitive need limits" (CNLs) that require the President to automatically suspend GSP treatment for BDCs (LDBDCs and sub-Saharan beneficiaries are exempt) if imports of a product from a single country reach a specified threshold value ($140 million in 2009, $145 million in 2010, and $150 million in 2011), or if 50% or more of total U.S. imports of a product entering under the preference come from a single country.[49]

CNL waivers for products imported from BDCs may be granted on the basis of certain criteria. In deciding whether to grant a waiver, the President must (1) receive advice from the ITC as to whether a U.S. domestic industry could be adversely affected by the waiver; (2) determine that the waiver is in the U.S. economic interest; and (3) publish the determination in the Federal Register.[50] The President is also required to give "great weight" to the extent to which the BDC opens its markets and resources the United States, provides internationally recognized worker rights, and protects intellectual property rights.[51]

Waivers for BDCs may also be provided (in some cases automatically) if total U.S. imports of a product from all countries is small or "*de minimis*" (not to exceed $19 million in 2008 and $19.5 million in 2009),[52] or if the GSP-eligible article was not produced in the United States on January 1, 1995 (known as a 504(d) waiver).[53]

Table 1. Dutiable and Duty-Free Tariff Lines in Harmonized Tariff Schedule of the United States by Product Category

HTS Product Category	Total Tariff Lines in Category	MFN Duty-free Tariff Lines	Duty-free under GSP	Duty-free under GSP for LDC	Additional Duty-free under other trade preferences
Animal and plant products	1,096	304	282	402	16
Prepared food, beverages, spirits, tobacco	741	137	267	200	11
Chemicals and plastics	2,211	742	1,021	441	6
Wood and paper products	481	407	60	10	4
Textiles, leather, and footwear	1,320	257	176	30	223
Glassware, precious metals and stones, jewelry	388	144	177	51	6
Base metals and articles of base metals	855	491	321	41	2
Machinery, electronics, and high-tech apparatus	1,893	988	810	85	10
Aircraft, autos, and other transportation	240	123	77	40	0
Miscellaneous manufacturing	543	201	186	89	66
Fuels	72	41	7	24	0
Apparel	667	44	22	0	0
Totals	10,507	3,879	3,406	1,413	344

Source: U.S. General Accountability Office. International Trade: U.S. Trade Preference Programs Provide Important Benefits, But a More Integrated Approach Would Better Ensure that Programs Meet Shared Goals. GAO 08-443, March 2008.

Rules of Origin

Eligible goods under the U.S. GSP program must meet certain rules of origin (ROO) requirements in order to qualify for duty-free treatment. First, duty-free entry is only allowed if the article is imported directly from the beneficiary country into the United States. Second, at least 35% of the appraised value of the product must be the "growth, product or manufacture" of a beneficiary developing country, as defined by the sum of (1) the cost or value of materials produced in the beneficiary developing country (or any two or more beneficiary countries that are members of the same association or countries and are treated as one country for purposes of the U.S. law) plus (2) the direct costs of processing in the country.[54]

Annual Review

The U.S. GSP program is subject to annual review by the GSP Subcommittee of the Trade Policy Staff Committee (TPSC), a body chaired by the Office of the U.S. Trade Representative (USTR), and including representatives from the Departments of Agriculture, Commerce, the Interior, Labor, State, and the Treasury.[55] The GSP Subcommittee (also responsible for making initial country eligibility recommendations) considers and makes recommendations to the President concerning the continued eligibility of countries to receive benefits. The GSP Subcommittee also resolves questions regarding BDC's and LDBDC's observance of country practices (such as worker rights, or protection of intellectual property rights); investigates petitions to add or remove items from the list of eligible products; and considers which products should be removed on the basis that they are "sufficiently competitive" or "import sensitive." In preparation for the annual review, the USTR may also seek an investigation by the ITC for the purpose of providing advice concerning any possible modifications to the GSP.[56]

2009 Annual GSP Review Results[57]

Results of the 2009 annual review, as published in the Federal Register (Proclamation 8539 of June 29, 2010), included the following:

- Frozen beans (HTS 0710.22.40) and frozen vegetable mixtures (HTS 0710.90.91) were added to the list of eligible products for the GSP.
- A request for a CNL waiver for new pneumatic radial tires (HTS 4011.10.10) imported from Thailand was denied.
- Duty-free status was removed for gold mixed necklaces and neck chains (HTS 7113.19.25) imported from India. A CNL waiver previously granted to India for the same product was revoked.

Another type of gold neck chain (HTS 7113.19.21) from India reached the CNL threshold, therefore becoming ineligible for GSP status.

- Over 100 products were granted *de minimis* waivers (provided when U.S. imports of a product from all countries are small or *de minimis*), including products from Thailand, Ecuador, India, Brazil, Pakistan, and Uruguay.
- A request that certain types of sleeping bags (HTS 9494.30.80) be removed form GSP eligibility was denied.
- Investigations on country practice issues, such as worker rights (Bangladesh, Niger, Philippines, and Uzbekistan) and intellectual property violations (Lebanon, Philippines, Russia, Uzbekistan, Lebanon) were continued beyond the annual review date, with progress to be reviewed "in [a] specific timeframe." Two new investigation requests, one on worker rights in Sri Lanka and one on arbitral awards in Argentina, were accepted for review.

On July 15, 2010, the USTR announced the initiation of the 2010 annual product review and solicited petitions from the public.[58]

Graduation

The President may remove a beneficiary developing country from GSP eligibility because the country is determined to be sufficiently competitive or developed that it no longer requires GSP benefits.[59] The President may graduate a BDC completely, or may do so with respect to the country's individual products or industries. Mandatory country graduation occurs when the BDC is determined to be a "high income country" (as defined by official International Bank for Reconstruction and Development statistics), or as a result of a review of the BDC's advances in economic development and trade competitiveness.[60] In December 2009, the President announced the mandatory graduation of Equatorial Guinea and Croatia, effective January 1, 2011.[61]

Countries also become ineligible for GSP benefits if they formally enter into a bilateral trading relationship with another developed country.[62] Bulgaria and Romania were the last countries to become ineligible for this reason, "effective for each of the countries when it becomes a European Member State" as of January 1, 2007 (Presidential Proclamation 8098, December 29, 2007).[63]

LEGISLATION IN THE 111TH CONGRESS

In previous years that the GSP was set to expire, its subsequent renewal was generally considered non-controversial. At times that it was not renewed prior to repeal, it was widely expected that Congress would retroactively renew the preference as it did in the Trade Act of 2002.[64] Since its renewal in December 2006, however, the extension of the GSP program and other trade preferences continues to be a matter of some debate. Some in Congress have mentioned that certain "more advanced" developing countries (such as Brazil and India) are receiving GSP benefits to the exclusion of lesser-developed countries. The consideration of Vietnam as a potential GSP beneficiary — initially proposed by the Bush Administration—is also a matter of debate for some in Congress, largely due to concerns over the country's record on worker rights.[65]

GSP Extension

A measure seeking to extend the GSP for one year was introduced on December 11, 2009 (H.R. 4284), and passed the House under suspension of the rules on December 14. The measure subsequently passed the Senate on December 22 by unanimous consent, and was signed by the President on December 28, 2009. Reportedly the short-term extension was enacted so that Congress could continue to discuss possible legislative options for trade preference reform in the second session of the 111th Congress.[66]

On December 15, the House passed H.R. 6517, the Omnibus Trade Act of 2010, which sought to extend the GSP through June 30, 2012. On December 22, 2010, the Senate passed an amendment in the nature of a substitute to H.R. 6517 that did not include GSP renewal. The amended version was passed by the House on the same date (P.L. 111-344). Therefore, the GSP program expired effective December 31, 2010. Thus, renewal of GSP may continue to be a legislative issue for the 112th Congress.

GSP for Vietnam

Two related bills sought to prohibit the President from granting Vietnam GSP status. H.R. 1969, the Vietnam Human Rights Act of 2009, would have required the President certifies to Congress that the government of Vietnam freely protects freedom of association in law and practice; and does not engage in or condone serious violations of worker rights, including detention, harassment, or arrest of labor activists or other individuals who write, speak, or otherwise disseminate information on worker rights before GSP status could have been granted. S. 1159 would have prohibited GSP for Vietnam would unless the President determined and certified that Vietnam (1) fully protects "in law and practice" freedom of association, including formation of labor unions and collective bargaining; (2) does not engage in or condone the harassment, detention, or arrest of labor activists; (3) fully protects "in law and practice" internationally recognized worker rights, including prohibitions on forced labor and a statutory minimum age for child labor; and (4) has released all people who were detained for peaceful activities promoting the rights of workers to freely associate, including the formation of trade unions.

OPIC Reauthorization

S. 705, the Overseas Private Investment Corporation (OPIC) Reauthorization Act of 2009, would have expanded OPIC project requirements so that it would not be able to "insure, reinsure, guaranty, or finance a project" unless the country in which the project is to be undertaken is eligible for designation as a BDC under the Generalized System of Preferences and the country has taken steps to afford its workers internationally recognized human rights, or the beneficiary country is not eligible for GSP designation but has take steps to grant worker rights protections. This bill was ordered to be reported favorably by the Senate Committee on Foreign Relations.

New Preferences

H.R. 4101, the New Partnership for Trade Development Act of 2009, sought to strengthen and improve the African Growth and Opportunity Act (AGOA), while extending similar enhanced trade benefits for other least-developed countries outside of Africa, such as Yemen, Afghanistan, and Bangladesh.

S. 1141, the Tariff Relief Assistance for Developing Economies Act of 2009, would have established a preference program similar to the GSP and AGOA, which would provide enhanced trade benefits for least-developed countries, including Yemen, Afghanistan, and Bangladesh.

EFFECTIVENESS OF GSP

The statutory goals of the GSP are (1) to promote the development of developing countries, (2) to promote trade, rather than aid, as a more efficient way of promoting economic development, (3) stimulate U.S. exports in developing country markets, and (4) promote trade liberalization in developing countries.[67] It is difficult to assess whether or not the program alone has achieved these goals, however, because the GSP is only one of many such foreign aid initiatives used by the United States to assist poorer countries. Economic success within countries is also related to internal factors, such as stability, wise policy decisions, availability of infrastructure to foster industry, and legal/financial frameworks that encourage foreign investment.

What follows, therefore, are general comments, rather than hard data, about the impact of GSP on developing countries, and possible economic effects on the U.S. market. The positions of various stakeholders regarding the value of the program are also discussed.

Effects on Developing Countries

In the last 10 years, total U.S. imports from all GSP beneficiaries have increased dramatically, from $150 billion in 2000 to a peak of $378 billion in 2008 (see Figure 1). In 2009, total imports from beneficiaries dropped to $241 billion—most likely due to the global economic recession. Growth in total imports could indicate, in very general terms, that the GSP and other preferential programs have helped create some export-driven growth in developing countries. Total exports entering duty-free under the GSP preference also increased markedly until 2008 from $16 billion in 2000 to $32 billion in 2008. From 2008 to 2009, the value of goods entering under GSP also fell to $20 billion.

However, the percentage of goods entering the United States under the GSP program, relative to total U.S. imports from BDCs, has remained relatively flat—at around 10% of total imports. This may be due, in part, to the presence of the automatic CNLs on GSP-eligible products, combined with mandatory graduation from the program.

Source: ITC Trade Dataweb.

Figure 1. U.S. Imports from GSP Countries.

Another indicator of the GSP's impact on developing countries is the utilization rate of the preference. At first glance, it seems that only a few beneficiary developing countries use GSP to a great extent. However, as one study pointed out, the apparent lack of utilization masks the fact that many GSP-eligible goods may also be imported duty-free under other U.S. regional preference schemes, such as AGOA.[68] The study also illustrated that, for certain industries in BDCs, the positive impact of GSP is quite significant. For example, for all agricultural commodities eligible for GSP treatment, the GSP utilization rate was approximately 58%.[69] Therefore, for individual industries in developing countries, the positive impact of the GSP could be seen as quite significant.

Many developing countries with a natural competitive advantage in certain products use trade preferences such as the GSP to gain a foothold in the international market. For example, India and Thailand have well-established jewelry industries, and Argentina enjoys an advantage in certain leather goods that are imported under the preference. Exporters in these industries have been able to expand their international reach through GSP programs. However, some countries may be encouraged by preferential programs to develop industry sectors where they would otherwise never be able to compete, thus diverting resources from other industries that might actually become competitive over time (trade diversion).[70] Although economic theory holds that trade diversion is not without efficiency costs, empirical evidence suggests that the overall effects of GSP are relatively small.[71]

The lack of reciprocity in the GSP program could also result in long-term costs for beneficiary countries. In multilateral trade negotiations, such as the Doha Development Round, countries may engage in reciprocal tariff reductions, meaning that all parties would agree to reduce their tariffs. By avoiding such reciprocal concessions, some developing countries may have tended to keep in place trade policies that may, in fact, impede their long-term growth. Moreover, these preferences can become an impediment to negotiations as developing countries seek ways of maintaining their preferences from eroding.

For this reason, some economists prefer multilateral, nondiscriminatory tariff cuts because preferential tariff programs, such as the GSP, can lead to inefficient production and trade patterns. When tariffs are reduced across-the-board, rather than in a preferential manner, countries tend to produce and export on the basis of their comparative advantage—thus exporting products that they produce relatively efficiently and importing products that others produce relatively efficiently. However, while some developing country producers (especially those whose products do not qualify under GSP) may benefit from multilateral tariff reductions, other industries may be hurt because their margin of preference under GSP is reduced.

Economic Effects on the U.S. Market

Imports under the GSP program in 2009 represented about $20.3 billion, in comparison to total U.S. imports of $1.5 trillion (imports for consumption, customs value). This might indicate that the overall effects of GSP on the U.S. economy are quite small. In addition, while U.S. imports from GSP countries has grown rapidly, the rate of increase of imports actually entering under the GSP program has, in the past 10 years, been relatively flat (see *Figure 1*). This factor could indicate that there may be little impact on the U.S. market as a whole by extending the preference. In federal budgetary terms, the Congressional Budget Office (CBO) estimated that, were the GSP to be extended from 2007 to 2011, revenue losses through forgone tariff receipts would amount to about $3.1 billion.[72]

In addition, U.S. producers of import-competing products are largely protected from severe economic impact. First, certain products, such as most textile and apparel products, are designated "import sensitive" and therefore ineligible for duty-free treatment. Second, "competitive need limits" (discussed in more detail above) are triggered when imports of a product from a single country reach a specified threshold value or when 50% of total U.S. imports of a product come from a single country.[73] Third, U.S. producers may petition the USTR that GSP treatment granted to eligible articles be withdrawn.[74] The fact that, as illustrated in *Figure 1*, the dollar amount of imports entering under GSP has remained fairly level for at least the past 10 years may also indicate that the GSP has little impact on most domestic producers.

Some U.S. manufacturers and importers also benefit from the lower cost of consumer goods and raw materials imported under the GSP program. U.S. demand for certain individual products, such as jewelry, leather, and aluminum, is quite significant.[75] However, it is difficult to gauge, other than anecdotally, the overall impact of the GSP program on the U.S. market when compared to similar imports from other countries that do not receive the preference. It is possible that some merchandise entering under the GSP could be competitive even without the preference, but it is also possible that the duty-free status is the primary factor that makes imports from these countries more attractive.

Stakeholders' Concerns

Supporters of the GSP include beneficiary developing country governments and exporters, U.S. importers, and some U.S. manufacturers who use inputs entering under GSP in downstream products. Some policymakers favor GSP renewal because they believe it is an important development and foreign policy tool. Those who oppose the program include U.S. producers who manufacture competing products and some in Congress who favor more reciprocal approaches to trade policy. What follows is a thematic approach to the major topics of discussion in the GSP renewal debate.

"Special and Differential Treatment"

Developing countries have long maintained that "special and differential treatment," such as that provided by the GSP, is an important assurance of access to U.S. and other developed country markets in the midst of increasing globalization.[76] Many of these countries have built industries (or segments of industries) based on receiving certain tariff preferences.

Those who oppose automatic renewal of GSP have expressed the desire to see some "reciprocity" and "appreciation" on the part of BDCs—in the form of offers of improved market access—in return for renewal of the program.[77] Some of these policy makers favor continued progress in bilateral or multilateral negotiations in lieu of extending automatic, nonreciprocal benefits such as the GSP. Others have also charged some of the more advanced BDCs for obstructing multilateral trade talks, especially in the WTO Doha Round.

Some Members are reportedly becoming more skeptical about the efficacy of any further trade concessions as they hear from constituents about lost jobs and other domestic hardships attributed to global competition.[78] Other Members believe that extension and expansion of these programs "will send a signal to developing countries that we will stand with them as they grow."[79]

Erosion of Preferential Margins

Developing countries have expressed concern about the overall progressive erosion[80] of preferential margins as a result of across-the-board tariff negotiations within the context of multilateral trade negotiations such as the Doha Round. In 1997, a study prepared by the Organization for Economic Cooperation and Development (OECD) found that the degree of erosion of preferences resulting from Uruguay Round (1986-1994) tariff concessions by the Quad countries (Canada, European Union, Japan, United States) was indeed significant.[81] Some economists point out that if multilateral rounds of tariff reductions continue, the preference may disappear completely unless GSP tariff headings are expanded to include more "import-sensitive" products.[82]

One example of present concern of preference erosion is the aforementioned group of business and NGO groups that have proposed providing duty-free, quota-free (DFQF) U.S. market access to all least-developed countries. Many sub-Saharan African countries have expressed concern that an approach like this could place them in direct competition for U.S. market share with countries like Bangladesh, thus diluting the value of the preferential treatment that they receive through the African Growth and Opportunity Act (AGOA).[83]

Other economists say that preference erosion could be more than outweighed by the benefits of increased market access, even for developing countries, brought about by multilateral trade liberalization.[84] These economists say that, rather than continuing GSP and other preferential programs (either through inertia or concern that removing them would be seen as "acting against" the world's poorest populations), a better approach might be to "assist them in addressing the constraints that really underlie their sluggish trade and growth performance."[85]

Under-Utilization of GSP

Some who oppose the program say that the proportionately small amount of trade entering under the GSP means that the program is underused, and therefore easily eliminated. Some supporters agree that this is especially true for many least-developed country beneficiaries, who historically are not large users of the preference.

Others have suggested that the GSP may not be used by some countries because they are unfamiliar with the program, because some BDC governments do a poor job of promoting the existence of available opportunities under the preference, because of the lack of available infrastructure (for example, undeveloped or damaged roads and ports that impede the efforts to get goods into the international market), or a combination of all of these factors.[86] One option for addressing these factors is assistance through U.S. trade capacity building efforts.

Trade as Foreign Assistance

No other U.S. preference program is more broadly based or encompasses as many countries as the GSP. As a result, the GSP program is supported by many observers who believe that it is an effective, low-cost means of providing economic assistance to developing countries. They maintain that encouraging trade by private companies through the GSP stimulates economic development much more effectively than intergovernmental aid and other means of assistance.[87] Economic development assistance through trade is a long-standing element of U.S. policy, and other trade promotion programs such as the AGOA and the Caribbean Basin Trade Partnership Act (CBTPA) are also based on this premise.

One example of support for GSP renewal occurred in April 2009, when a coalition of nongovernmental organizations (NGOs) working to reduce world poverty and U.S. businesses interested in including developing countries in their sourcing plans, urged USTR Ron Kirk to "seek timely renewal of expiring preference programs for those countries found to fulfill each program's eligibility criteria and to initiate review and reform of existing U.S. preference programs."[88] The coalition mentioned that preference programs, like GSP, help to spur much-needed economic development and opportunity, and that quick renewal could help cushion beneficiary countries from the economic impact brought about by declines in trade flows during the global economic crisis.[89] The coalition also spoke to the effectiveness of preference programs in helping to address development challenges while taking into account the needs of U.S. companies and workers.[90]

Conditionality of Preferences

Some supporters of the GSP and other non-reciprocal preferences believe that the conditions required (such as worker rights and intellectual property requirements) for GSP qualification provide the United States with international political leverage that can be used to preserve U.S. foreign and commercial interests.[91] However, some beneficiary countries actively object to these "country practice" provisions and regard them as penalties. Some countries (such as Brazil and India), that have been targeted for GSP eligibility review in the past, perceive that such action indicates that they are being penalized for advocating for their own national development goals in multilateral talks.[92]

Some U.S. intellectual property industry representatives, worker rights groups, and other constituencies oppose what they perceive to be the U.S. administration's inconsistent enforcement of these provisions. For example, one lobbying group expressed that they were "shocked and dumbfounded" that the GSP is being annually renewed for such countries as Brazil, Russia, and Venezuela in spite of intellectual property rights violations.[93] This domestic opposition may indicate that, at times, the GSP as a tool is of limited usefulness. According to the USTR, however, U.S. officials favor working with beneficiary countries during country practice reviews to actively address compliance issues before removing a country from eligibility. Between 2001 and 2006, one country was removed from eligibility for GSP because of intellectual property rights concerns but was reinstated a few years later after taking steps to resolve the problem.[94]

Lower Costs of Imports

U.S. importers of goods who import components, parts, or materials duty-free under the GSP maintain that the preference results in lower costs for these intermediate goods which, in turn, can be passed on to consumers. In a May 1, 2006, letter to the House Ways and Means and Senate Finance Committees, a coalition of importers and retailers warned that if the GSP was allowed to expire, or if its benefits were reduced, it "would impose a costly hardship on not only beneficiary countries, but their American customers as well."[95] Industry representatives mentioned that smaller domestic manufacturers who regularly import inputs under the preference may be especially affected by a lapse or expiration of the program because they are less able to adjust to the increased costs that would result.[96]

Even though most U.S. producers are shielded by the automatic safeguards triggered by increased imports under the GSP, some U.S. manufacturers and workers might be adversely affected by the program due to CNL waivers.[97] For example, in 2004, three U.S. producers of titanium complained that the Bush Administration refused to terminate duty-free market access for wrought titanium (ordinarily subject to a 15% duty assessment), despite a petition asking the government not to waive the import limits. Russian imports of titanium were allowed to continue to enter duty-free under the Presidential waiver even though its sales made up more than 60% of U.S. imports.[98] This might be seen by some as another inconsistency in administration of the U.S. program.

CONCLUSION AND OPTIONS FOR CONGRESS

The U.S. GSP program, as established by Title V of the Trade Act of 1974, was last extended for all countries through December 31, 2010, in P.L. 111-124. Congress may once again consider its extension (and that of other trade preference programs set to expire), during the 112th Congress. The African Growth and Opportunity Acceleration Act of 2004 (P.L. 108-274) had previously authorized an extension of GSP preferences for all beneficiary developing sub-Saharan African countries under the African Growth and Opportunity Act (AGOA) through September 30, 2015, therefore, whether or not the GSP program is renewed with respect to other countries, GSP benefits will continue to be extended to all AGOA countries.[99]

Several options are available to Congress with respect to the treatment of the GSP program. As explained more fully below, Congress could allow the GSP program to expire, support reciprocal tariff and market access benefits through free trade agreements, renew the GSP for least-developed beneficiaries only, renew the existing program for all beneficiaries without major amendments, or extend the program in a modified form. Although the GSP is a unilateral and non-reciprocal tariff preference, any changes to the program would need to be considered in light of the requirements of the WTO Enabling Clause, as it has been interpreted by the WTO Appellate Body. At a minimum, the United States would need to notify – and possibly consult – with other WTO Members regarding any withdrawal or modification of GSP benefits, as required by paragraph 4 of the Clause. The United States could also pursue a WTO waiver were any modifications of the GSP program considered not to comport fully with U.S. WTO obligations.

Allow GSP to Expire

The GSP statute will automatically expire for all beneficiary developing countries (except AGOA-eligible countries) on December 31, 2010.[100] No legislative action would be required if Congress were to allow the expiration of GSP for BDCs and LDBDCS not otherwise granted GSP benefits through other preferential programs (such as AGOA).

Some in Congress have asserted that if the GSP were not renewed, it could spur positive movement in the DDA. This position was presented during the 2006 renewal debate by then-House Ways and Means Chairman Representative Bill Thomas and then-Senate Finance Committee Chairman Senator Charles Grassley.[101] A similar position was also advocated in early 2002 when, while testifying on intellectual property issues, then-USTR Robert B. Zoellick mentioned that "the threat of loss of GSP ... benefits has proven to be an effective point of leverage with some of our trading partners."[102]

Other observers indicate that if GSP were allowed to expire, or be otherwise modified through country graduation or limitations on CNL waivers, these actions might also weaken the hand of U.S. negotiators in the DDA because GSP could no longer be used as an incentive for participation. Many developing nations already perceive the United States as generally unwilling to accept multilateral efforts to grant additional "special and differential treatment" for developing country WTO members (an important DDA goal) unless more reciprocal concessions for improved market access are made for U.S. products. As a result, GSP expiration could cause the negotiating positions of developing countries to harden, rather than soften, as they seek to make up for these lost benefits through the negotiations.

These observers say that the United States could also lose substantial leverage in addressing important trade-related foreign policy and development concerns that beneficiary nations must accept prior to BDC designation. Furthermore, interested domestic and international parties may now file petitions requesting the USTR to review the GSP status of BDCs based on the eligibility criteria in the statute (e.g., worker rights practices). If the GSP program were no longer in effect, these avenues of encouraging certain developing country practices would no longer be available.[103]

Some domestic manufacturers, such as the ailing U.S. automobile industry, may be additionally impacted by GSP expiration or modification, due to dependence on duty-free (thus lower-cost) manufacturing inputs imported under the preference, such as brake parts, vehicle transmissions, and tires. Smaller businesses could be disproportionately affected because they are less able to adjust to increased costs of factors of production. On the other hand, some U.S. manufacturers of import-competing products might, at least marginally, benefit.

Scrap GSP in Favor of Free-Trade Agreements or Regional Trading Arrangements

Some Members of Congress have suggested that the GSP should be abandoned in favor of free trade agreements (FTAs) or regional trading arrangements (RTAs) that would provide the United States with reciprocal benefits. Such arrangements could provide additional markets for U.S. exports, as well as stimulate the growth of industries in developing-country trading partners. Thus, U.S. exporters, as well as importers, could benefit from reciprocal tariff concessions. Since these tariff concessions under these agreements would probably apply to many more goods and industries than are covered by the existing GSP program, they might increase the likelihood of across-the-board economic stimulation in the developing country trading partner. In addition, absent a favorable conclusion to the DDA negotiations, FTAs and RTAs could also be used as a way to lead countries toward further multilateral trade liberalization.

However, such reciprocal agreements could actually harm import-competing U.S. manufacturers more than unilateral preferences under the GSP, because automatic safeguards written into the statute, such as competitive need limitations, might no longer apply. Any such agreement could also involve a greater number of U.S. tariff concessions, thus certain import-sensitive items ineligible for GSP status could also be on the table. On the other hand, other U.S. manufacturers might benefit from the increased market access that an FTA or RTA would provide.

Some developing countries could also be put at a greater disadvantage in free-trade or regional-trade agreement negotiations because they are ill-equipped to implement the additional standards that accompany a comprehensive U.S. free trade agreement.[104] For example, some countries such as South Africa and other countries in the South African Customs Union

(SACU) have been unsuccessful in the past when negotiating such agreements with the United States due to their inability to conform to these standards. In addition, since the GSP is the largest U.S. preferential trading program, some developing countries that currently receive GSP benefits could easily be left out of such agreements, either because their markets are of little commercial value to U.S. interests, or because time constraints involved in the negotiating process do not make it worthwhile for U.S. negotiators to include them.

Authorize GSP Only for Least-Developed Countries

Some in Congress favor modifying the GSP so that it applies only with respect to least-developed beneficiaries. Since many African least-developed beneficiaries will continue to receive the GSP preference until mid-2015 under AGOA, an LDC-only GSP extension would apply to the following LDCs: Afghanistan, Bangladesh, Bhutan, Cambodia, Central African Republic, Congo (Kinshasa), Haiti,[105] Kiribati, Madagascar, Nepal, Samoa, The Solomon Islands, Somalia, Tuvalu, Vanuatu, and Yemen.

Of these countries, only four (Bhutan, Congo (Kinshasa), Samoa, and Nepal) currently export goods under GSP that account for more than 8% of their total imports to the United States. Therefore, if the GSP program were to be renewed and extended to LDCs only (absent any other modifications), these four countries would be the primary beneficiaries in the short term. Arguably, U.S. efforts through trade capacity building could help other LDCs take greater advantage of the preference.

Modify GSP

Another possible approach for Congress would be to modify the Generalized System of Preferences scheme as it applies to all beneficiary developing countries, including least-developed countries. Some of these options would have the effect of narrowing the application of the GSP program, while others would expand it.

Restrict Application of Preference

The following is a list of possible approaches if Congress desired to extend, but further restrict, imports under the GSP:

- Refine statutory criteria for GSP treatment. For example, make the existing discretionary criteria mandatory requirements.
- Strengthen the requirement that benefits under the preference may (or must) be terminated for non-compliance with mandatory or discretionary criteria. Add additional criteria to include movement toward sustainable development or environmental preservation.
- Reconsider criteria for graduation of countries from GSP, or strengthen the provision that allows graduation of individual industries within beneficiary countries. For example, the President could be required to grant BDC status only if a country (1) complies with all mandatory requirements and (2) has a per-capita income below a certain level.
- Modify the rules of origin requirement for qualifying products to require that a greater percentage of the direct costs of processing operations (currently 35%)[106] originate in beneficiary developing countries.
- Lower the threshold at which the President may (or must) withdraw, suspend, or limit the application of duty-free treatment of certain products (competitive need limitation).[107]
- Require the President to more frequently and actively monitor (currently an annual process) the economic progress of beneficiary countries, as well as compliance with mandatory and discretionary criteria.
- Weed out countries considered "unfriendly" to U.S. interests, such as Venezuela, India, and Brazil.

Expand Application of GSP

Were Congress to expand or enhance application of the GSP, the following options could be exercised:

- Expand the list of tariff lines permitted duty-free access. Allow some "import sensitive" products (in which developing countries often have a competitive advantage) to receive preferential access.
- Improve rule of origin requirements to provide more predictability. Current rules provide no measurable definition of "substantial transformation," therefore, U.S. officials often make eligibility decisions on a case-by-case basis; therefore BDCs sometimes have no predictable way of knowing before shipment whether certain foreign components can be included as part of the 35% domestic content.[108]

- Eliminate competitive need limitations or raise the thresholds that trigger them.
- Ensure uniform application of country practice requirements, or eliminate them.

APPENDIX A. TRADE STATISTICS

Table A-1. Leading Product Imports Under GSP, 2009

HTS	MFN Tariff Rate	Description	Value of Imports Under GSP
2709002090	10.5 cents/bbl	Petroleum oils and oils from bituminous minerals, crude, testing 25 degrees A.P.I. or more	$5,418,587,736
2709001000	5.25 cents/bbl	Petroleum oils and oils from bituminous minerals, crude, testing under 25 degrees A.P.I.	$605.585,126
7113115080	5%	Silver articles of jewelry and parts thereof, nesoi, valued over $18 per dozen pieces or parts	$493,043,718
2709002010	10.5 cents/bbl	Condensate derived wholly from natural gas	$457,242,613
7113192980	5.5%	Necklaces and neck chains, of gold, not otherwise specified or indicated	$185,968,143
7606123090	3%	Aluminum plates, sheets and strip, rectangular, including sq. alloy, not clad, with a thickness of 6.3 mm or less, not otherwise specified or indicated	$154,175,080
1701111000	1.4606¢/kg less 0.020668¢/kg for each degree under 100 degrees (and fractions of a degree in proportion) but not less than 0.943854¢/kg	Cane sugar, raw, in solid form, not containing added flavoring or coloring matter, not otherwise specified or indicated, described in additional U.S. note 5 (Chapter 17) and provisional	$149,431,537
4011101040	4%	Radial tires with rim diameter greater than 15" but less than 16"	$122,025,388

Table A-1. (Continued).

HTS	MFN Tariff Rate	Description	Value of Imports Under GSP
8504230080	1.6%	Liquid dielectric transformers having a power handling capacity exceeding 100,000 KVA	$120,087,655
6802990060	6.5%	Other stone, not otherwise specified or indicated	$117,947,979
9001500000	2%	Spectacle lenses of other materials, uncounted	$117,705,354
7202410000	1.9%	Ferrochromium over 4 percent carbon	$112,331,832
4015191010	3%	Seamless disposable gloves, of vulcanized rubber other than hard rubber	$110,217,197
4011101030	4%	Radial tires with rim diameter greater than 14" but less than 15"	$102,150,945

Source: USITC Trade Dataweb, httpi/dataweb.usitc.gov, and Harmonized Tariff Schedule, 2009.

Notes: Imports for consumption, actual U.S. dollars. Tariff rates are *ad valorem* unless otherwise specified.

Table A-2. Leading GSP Beneficiaries and Total, 2009

Rank	Beneficiary Developing Country	GSP Duty-Free Imports ($ millions)	Total Imports ($ millions)
1	Angola	$4,142	$9,306
2	Thailand	$2,886	$18,964
3	India	$2,848	$21,228
4	Brazil	$1,978	$19, 612
5	Equatorial Guinea	$1,677	$2,391
6	Indonesia	$1,455	$12, 917
7	South Africa	$742	$5,877
8	Philippines	$734	$6,792
9	Turkey	$644	$3,649
10	Argentina	$506	$3,821
11	Chad	$486	$1,879
12	Russia	$252	$17,420
13	Congo (DROC)	$209	$318
14	Colombia	$189	$11,209
15	Pakistan	$169	$3,156
Imports from Top 15 Beneficiaries		$18,917	$138,539
Total Imports from all Beneficiaries		$20,228	$241,496

APPENDIX B. GSP IMPLEMENTATION AND RENEWAL

Table B-1. GSP Implementation and Renewal 1975-2009

Public Law	Effective Date	Date Expired	Notes
P.L. 93-618, Title V, Trade Act of 1974	January 2, 1975	January 2, 1985	Statute originally enacted.
P.L. 98-573, Title V, Trade and Tariff Act of 1984	October 30, 1984	July 4, 1993	Substantially amended and restated.
P.L. 103-66, Section 13802 (in Omnibus Budget Reconciliation Act, 1993)	August 10, 1993	September 30, 1994	Extended retroactively from July 5, 1993 to August 10, 1993. Also struck out reference to "Union of Soviet Socialist Republics"
P.L. 103-465, Section 601 Uruguay Round Agreements Act	December 8, 1994	July 31, 1995	Extended retroactively from September 30, 1994 to December 8, 1994. No other amendments to provision.
P.L. 104-188, Subtitle J, section 1952 GSP Renewal Act of 1996 (in Small Business Job Protection Act of 1996)	October 1, 1996 (for GSP renewal only)	May 31, 1997	Substantially amended and restated. Extended retroactively from August 1, 1995 to October 1, 1996.
P.L. 105-34, Subtitle H, section 981 (in Taxpayer Relief Act of 1997)	August 5, 1997	June 30, 1998	Extended retroactively from May 31, 1997 to August 5, 1997. No other amendments to provision.
P.L. 105-277, Subtitle B, section 101 (in Omnibus Consolidated and Emergency Supplemental Appropriations, 1999)	October 21, 1998	June 30, 1999	Extended retroactively from July 1, 1998 to October 21, 1998. No other amendments to provision.
P.L. 106-170, section 508, (in Ticket to Work and Work Incentives Act of 1999)	December 17, 1999	September 30, 2001	Extended retroactively from July 1, 1999 to December 17, 1999. No other amendments to provision.
P.L. 107-210, Division D, Title XLI Trade Act of 2002	August 6, 2002	December 31, 2006	Extended retroactively from September 30, 2001 to August 6, 2002. Amended to (1) include requirement that BDCs take steps to support efforts of United States to combat terrorism and (2) further define the term "internationally recognized worker rights."
P.L. 109-432, Title VIII	December 31, 2006	December 31, 2008	Extended before program lapse.
P.L. 110-436, section 4	October 16, 2008	December 31, 2009	Extended before program lapse.
P.L. 111-124	December 28, 2009	December 31, 2010	Extended before program lapse.

Appendix C. GSP Beneficiary Countries

Table C-1. Beneficiary Developing Countries and Regions for Purposes of the Generalized System of Preferences (GSP), and Additional Qualifying Preference Programs, January 2011

Individual Countries (columns continued on next page)		
Afghanistan A+	Guyana E	Seychelles G
Albania	Haiti A+ E	Sierra Leone A+ G
Algeria	India	Solomon Islands
Angola A+ G	Indonesia	Somalia A+
Argentina	Iraq	South Africa G
Armenia	Jamaica E	Sri Lanka
Azerbaijan	Jordan	Suriname
Bangladesh A+	Kazakhstan	Swaziland G
Belize E	Kenya G	Tanzania A+ G
Benin A+ G	Kiribati A+	Thailand
Bhutan A+	Kosovo	Togo A+ G
Bolivia J	Kyrgyzstan	Tonga
Bosnia and Hercegovina	Lebanon	Tunisia
Botswana G	Lesotho A+ G	Turkey
Brazil	Liberia A+ G	Tuvalu A+
Burkina Faso A+ G	Macedonia, Former Yugoslav	Uganda A+ G
	Republic of	
Burundi A+ G	Madagascar A+ G	Ukraine
Cambodia A+	Malawi A+ G	Uruguay
Cameroon G	Maldives	Uzbekistan
Cape Verde G	Mali A+ G	Vanuatu A+
Central African Republic A+	Mauritania A+	Venezuela
Chad A+ G	Mauritius G	Republic of Yemen A+
Colombia J	Moldova	Zambia A+ G
Comoros A+ G	Mongolia	Zimbabwe
Congo (Brazzaville) G	Montenegro	
Congo (Kinshasa) A+ G	Mozambique A+ G	
Cote d'Ivoire	Namibia G	
Djibouti A+ G	Nepal A+	
Dominica E	Niger A+ G	
	Nigeria G	
	Pakistan	
East Timor A+	Panama E	

Ecuador J	Papua New Guinea	
Egypt	Paraguay	
Eritrea	Philippines	
Ethiopia A+ G	Russia	
Fiji	Rwanda A+ G	
Gabon G	St. Kitts and Nevis E	
Gambia, The A+ G	Saint Lucia E	
Georgia	Saint Vincent and the Grenadines E	
Ghana G	Samoa A+	
Grenada E	Sao Tome and Principe A+	
Guinea A+ G	Senegal G	
Guinea-Bissau A+ G	Serbia	
Non-Independent Countries and Territories		
Anguilla	Gibraltar	Saint Helena
British Indian Ocean Territory	Heard Island and McDonald Islands	Tokelau
Christmas Island (Australia)	Montserrat E	Turks and Caicos Islands
Cocos (Keeling) Islands	Niue	Virgin Islands, British E
Cook Islands	Norfolk Island	Wallis and Fortuna
Falkland Islands (Islas Malvinas)	Pitcairn Islands	West Bank and Gaza Strip Western Sahara

Source: Harmonized Tariff Schedule of the United States, 2009.

Note: Symbols for Trade Preference Programs:

A+ = GSP Least-Developed Beneficiary Developing Country

J = Beneficiary Country of Andean Trade Preference (ATPA)

E = Beneficiary Country of Caribbean Basin Economic Trade Partnership Act (CBTPA) and/or Caribbean Basin Economic Recovery Act (CBERA). Additional beneficiaries of CBERA that have previously graduated from the GSP are Antigua and Barbuda, Aruba, Bahamas, Barbados, Netherlands Antilles, and Trinidad and Tobago.

G = Beneficiary Country of African Growth and Opportunity Act (AGOA).

Associations of Countries (treated as one country)	
Member Countries of the Cartagena	Qualifying Member Countries of the Southern Africa
Agreement (Andean Group)	Development Community (SADC)
Bolivia	Botswana
Colombia	Mauritius
Ecuador	Tanzania
Peru	Qualifying Member Countries of the South Asian
Member Countries of the West African	Association for Regional Cooperation (SAARC)
Economic and Monetary Union (WAEMU)	Bangladesh
Benin	Bhutan
Burkina Faso	India
Cote d'Ivoire	Nepal
Guinea-Bissau	Pakistan
Mali	Sri Lanka
Niger	Qualifying Member Countries of the Caribbean
Senegal	Common Market (CARICOM)
Togo	Belize
Qualifying Member Countries of the	Dominica
Association of South East Asian Nations	Grenada
(ASEAN)	Guyana
Cambodia	Jamaica
Indonesia	Montserrat
Philippines	St. Kitts and Nevis
Thailand	Saint Lucia
	Saint Vincent and the Grenadines
	Trinidad and Tobago

Source: Harmonized Tariff Schedule of the United States, 2009.

End Notes

[1] 19 U.S.C. § 2466b, as amended by section 7 of the AGOA Acceleration Act of 2004 (P.L. 108-274). AGOAdesignated countries in 2009 are Angola, Benin, Botswana, Burkina Faso, Burundi, Cameroon, Cape Verde, Chad, Comoros, Congo (DROC), Congo (ROC), Djibouti, Ethiopia, Gabon, Gambia, Ghana, Guinea, Guinea-Bissau, Kenya, Lesotho, Liberia, Madagascar, Malawi, Mali, Mauritius, Mozambique, Namibia, Niger, Nigeria, Rwanda, Sao Tome and Principe, Senegal, Seychelles, Sierra Leone, South Africa, Swaziland, Tanzania, Togo, Uganda, Zambia.

[2] U.N. Conference on Trade and Development, "About GSP," at http://www.unctad.org. In addition to the United States, the European Union and 11 other developed countries—Australia, Belarus, Bulgaria, Canada, Japan, New Zealand, Norway, Switzerland, and the Russian Federation—currently have GSP programs.

[3] OECD Secretary-General. *The Generalized System of Preferences: Review of the First Decade*. Organization of Economic Cooperation and Development, 1983, p. 9 (hereinafter OECD GSP Review).

[4] Ibid.

[5] Sapir, A. and L. Lundberg, "The U.S. Generalized System of Preferences and its Impacts," in R. Baldwin and A. Krueger (eds.) The Structure and Evolution of Recent U.S. Trade Policy, Chicago: The University of Chicago Press, 1984.

[6] The most-favored-nation principle means that countries must treat imports from other trading partners on the same basis as that given to the most favored other nation. Therefore, with certain exceptions (including GSP, regional trading arrangements, and free trade agreements), every country gets the lowest tariff that any country gets, and reductions in tariffs to one country are provided also to others. The term "most-favored-nation" has been changed in U.S. law to "normal trade relations."

[7] OECD GSP Review, p. 11.

[8] Ibid., p. 10.

[9] Wall, David. "Problems with Preferences." *International Affairs*, vol. 47, October 1971, p. 95.

[10] World Trade Organization. Ministerial Declaration, Annex F. December 18, 2005, WT/MIN(05)/DEC.

[11] Ibid.

[12] This section was written by Jeanne J. Grimmett, Legislative Attorney, American Law Division. For further discussion of trade preference programs in light of obligations under the General Agreement on Tariffs and Trade (GATT), see CRS Report RS22183, *Trade Preferences for Developing Countries and the World Trade Organization (WTO)*, by Jeanne J. Grimmett [hereinafter CRS Report RS22183, *Trade Preferences for Developing Countries and the World Trade Organization (WTO)*].

[13] Edmond McGovern, International Trade Regulation 9.212 (updated 1999). Part IV is generally viewed as nonbinding, though some have argued otherwise with regard to certain of its provisions. *Id.*; John H. Jackson, William J. Davey & Alan O. Sykes, Jr., Legal Problems of International Economic Relations 1171 (4th ed. 2002).

[14] GATT, Generalized System of Preferences; Decision of 25 June 1971, L/3545 (June 28, 1971), available at http://www.wto.org/gatt_docs/English/SULPDF/90840258.pdf.

[15] GATT, Differential and More Favourable Treatment, Reciprocity and Fuller Participation of Developing Countries; Decision of 28 November 1979, L/4903 (December 3, 1979)(footnotes omitted)(hereinafter Enabling Clause), available at http://www.wto.org /gatt_docs/English/SULPDF/90970166.pdf

[16] Id. 2, n.3.

[17] Id. 4, n.1.

[18] Note also notification requirements under 4 of the Enabling Clause, discussed in the text. See generally Simon Lester, *The Asian Newly Industrialized Countries to Graduate from Europe's GSP Tariffs*, 36 Harv. Int'l L. J. 220 (1995); Gregory O. Lunt, *Graduation and the GATT: The Problem of the NICs*, 31 Colum. J. Transnat'l L. 611 (1994); Robert E. Hudec, *GATT and the Developing Countries*, 1992 Colum. Bus. L. Rev. 67.

[19] Enabling Clause, *supra* note 15, at 2, n.2.

[20] CRS Report RS22183, *Trade Preferences for Developing Countries and the World Trade Organization (WTO)*, *supra* note 12, at 3. On May 27, 2009, the WTO General Council approved U.S. requests for waiver renewals for two non-GSP preference programs and an initial waiver for a third program, this being the final WTO action needed for the waivers to enter into effect. The waiver renewals cover the Caribbean Basin Economic Recovery Act (as amended by the United States-Caribbean Trade Partnership Act) and the Andean Trade Preference Act (as amended by the Andean Trade Promotion and Drug Eradication Act), each through December 31, 2014. Earlier waivers for these programs had expired in 2005 and 2001, respectively. The new waiver covers the African Growth and Opportunity Act through September 30, 2015. Some WTO Members (e.g., China and Pakistan), had expressed concerns regarding U.S. treatment of textiles in these programs, while Paraguay objected to the U.S. request in part because of its exclusion from the Andean preference scheme.

[21] Agreement Establishing the World Trade Organization, Annex 1A, General Agreement on Tariffs and Trade 1994, 1(b)(iv); see Appellate Body Report, *European Communities—Conditions for the Granting of Tariff Preferences to Developing Countries*, ¶ 90.3, WT/DS246/AB/R (April 7, 2004)(hereinafter EC Preferences AB Report).

[22] Preferential Tariff Treatment for Least-Developed Countries; Decision on Waiver, WT/L/304 (June 17, 1999) (adopted June 15, 1999), at http://docsonline.wto.org/DDFDocuments/t/WT/L/304.DOC; see also discussion in WTO Committee on Trade and Development, *Note on the Meeting of 2 March 1999*, at 2-6, WT/COMTD/M/24 (April 27, 1999).

[23] Preferential Tariff Treatment for Least-Developed Countries; Decision on Extension of Waiver, WT/L/759 (May 29, 2009)(adopted May 27, 2009).

[24] EC Preferences AB Report, *supra* note 21.

[25] Id. at 162-165. For further discussion of the Appellate Body report, *see* CRS Report RS22183, *Trade Preferences for Developing Countries and the World Trade Organization (WTO)*, supra note 12, at 4-5.

[26] Sanchez Arnau, Juan C. *The Generalized System of Preferences and the World Trade Organization*. London: Cameron May, Ltd., 2002, p. 187.

[27] Ibid.

[28] World Trade Organization. Committee on Trade and Development. The Generalized System of Preferences: A Preliminary Analysis of the GSP Schemes in the Quad. WTO Document WT/COMTD/W/93, October 5, 2001.

[29] United Nations Conference on Trade and Development. Generalized System of Preferences on the Scheme of Australia. UNCTAD Technical Cooperation Project on Market Access, Trade Laws and Preferences, June 2000 (INT/97/A06), p. 5. http://www.unctad.org/en/docs/itcdtsbmisc56_en.pdf.

[30] European Communities. See Council Regulation (EC) N Council Regulation (EC) No 732/2008 of 22 July 2008 applying a scheme of generalised tariff preferences for the period from 1 January 2009 to 31 December 2011 and amending Regulations (EC) No 552/97, (EC) No 1933/2006 and Commission Regulations (EC) No 1100/2006 and (EC) No 964/2007. Published in Official Journal of the European Communities (OJ) OJ L 211 of 6 August 2008. The "Everything but Arms" provision applies to all goods except arms and munitions, husked rice (80% of duties revoked until total suspension in September 2009), and white sugar (total suspension of duties planned for October 2009).

[31] Ibid.

[32] World Trade Organization. Committee on Trade and Development. *Notification by Japan* June 21, 2000, WT/COMTD/N/2/Add.9.

[33] Trade Act of 1974, P.L. 93-618, Title V, as amended, 19 U.S.C. § 2461-2467. The GSP Program was reauthorized and amended by the Trade and Tariff Act of 1984 (P.L. 98-573), and again by Subtitle J (the GSP Renewal Act of 1996) of P.L. 104-188. Six laws have authorized GSP with relatively minor modifications, most recently through December 31, 2006 (P.L. 107-210). See *Table B-1,* "GSP Implementation and Renewal 1975-2009."

[34] 19 U.S.C. § 2461.

[35] 19 U.S.C. § 2462.

[36] 19 U.S.C. § 2462(b). The most recent amendments required the support of U.S. efforts against terrorism and expanded the definition of internationally recognized worker rights (Section 4102 of P.L. 107-210). See also United States Trade Representative. *U.S. Generalized System of Preferences Guidebook*, January 2006, p. 19 (hereinafter USTR Guidebook).

[37] 19 U.S.C. § 2462(c). Ibid., p. 20.

[38] 19 U.S.C. §2462(d).

[39] 19 U.S.C. § 2462(d)(3).

[40] 19 U.S.C. § 2464.

[41] 19 U.S.C. § 2462(a)(2).

[42] 19 U.S.C. § 2462(c)(2).

[43] See 71 F.R. 43543.

[44] 19 U.S.C. § 2463(a)(1).

[45] 19 U.S.C. § 2463(b).

[46] The GSP Subcommittee is a sub-group of the Trade Policy Staff Committee, given jurisdiction over designating beneficiary countries and covered products in the GSP program in Executive Order 11846, 40 F.R. 14291, as amended.

[47] USTR Guidebook, p. 8.

[48] USTR Guidebook and *Table A-1,* Appendix A.

[49] 19 U.S.C. § 2463(c)(2)(A). See also USTR Guidebook, p. 10.

[50] 19 U.S.C. § 2463(d).

[51] 19 U.S.C. § 2463(d)(2).

[52] 19 U.S.C. § 2463(c)(2)(F).

[53] 19 U.S.C. § 2463(c)(2)(E).

[54] 19 U.S.C. § 2463(a).

[55] Regulations for implementation of the GSP program were issued by the Office of the United States Trade Representatives at 15 C.F.R. § 2007. Provisions for the GSP Annual Review are set out at 15 C.F.R. § 2007.2(c)-(h).

[56] 19 U.S.C. § 1332(g), 19 U.S.C. § 2463.

[57] Presidential Proclamation 8539 of June 29, 2010 (75 F.R. 38905); and United States Trade Representative, "Results of the 2009 GSP Annual Review," .

[58] 75 F.R. 41274.

[59] In this case, the discretionary eligibility criteria under 19 U.S.C. 2462(c)(2) applies.

[60] 19 U.S.C. § 2462(e).

[61] Presidential Proclamation 8467 of December 23, 2009, 74. F.R. 69221, December 30, 2009.

[62] Although not specifically stated in the statute, the United States has generally removed countries from GSP eligibility that sign FTAs with it as well.

[63] 72 F.R. 459. USTR officially announced the graduation of Bulgaria and Romania on January 22, 2007 (72 F.R. 2717).

[64] In each instance since 1993 (the last time that the program expired) it was allowed to lapse and was extended retroactively from the expiration date to the date of enactment. P.L. 107-210, for example, applied the preference to any goods entering the United States between September 30, 2001 and August 6, 2002. See *Table B-1,* "GSP Implementation and Renewal 1975-2009." The 2006 renewal (until December 2008) was the first time since 1993 that the program had not been allowed to lapse prior to renewal.

[65] CRS Report RL34702, *Potential Trade Effects of Adding Vietnam to the Generalized System of Preferences Program*, by Michael F. Martin and Vivian C. Jones

[66] "Senate Passes GSP, ATPDEA Extensions after Lautenberg Lifts Hold" *Inside U.S. Trade*, December 25, 2009.

[67] P.L. 98-573, section 501(b), 19 U.S.C. § 2461 note. Additional factors are to allow for differences in developing countries; help developing countries generate foreign exchange reserves, further integrate developing countries into the international trading system; and encourage developing countries to eliminate trade barriers, guard intellectual property rights, provide worker rights; and address concerns of the United States with regard to adverse effects on U.S. producers and workers and compliance with GATT obligations.

[68] Organization for Economic Cooperation and Development (OECD). *Agriculture and Food.* Preferential Trading Arrangements in Agricultural and Food Markets The Case of the European Union and the United States: United States Preference Schemes. Volume 2005, No. 1, p. 81. See also U.S. Government Accountability Office. *U.S. Trade Preference Programs Provide Important Benefits, but a More Integrated Approach Would Better Ensure Programs Meet Shared Goals*, March 2008, p. 19.

[69] Ibid.

[70] OECD. "Making Open Markets Work for Development." *Policy Brief*, October 2005, p. 2.

[71] Laird, Samuel and Andre Sapir. "Tariff Preferences." In Finger, J. Michael and Andrzej Olechowski, eds. *The Uruguay Round: A Handbook on the Multilateral Trade Negotiations*. Washington, World Bank, 1987, p. 105.

[72] Congressional Budget Office. *The Budget and Economic Outlook: Fiscal Years 2007 to 2016*, Table 4.10, "Effects of Extending Tax Provisions Scheduled to Expire Before 2016." CBO estimates that revenue losses would be $0.3 billion in FY2006, $0.6 billion in FY2007 and 0.7 billion in 2008 and 2009. Estimates are based on the assumption that the quantity of imports under the preference will increase over the term, but do not take into account any possible lowering of tariffs or reductions in value of imports.

[73] 19 U.S.C. § 2463(c).

[74] 15 C.F.R. 2007.0(b).

[75] In some product categories, imports under GSP account for 25% or more of total U.S. imports, including leather (45% of all U.S. leather imports), jewelry and jewelry parts (43%), ferroalloys (36%), copper wire (25%), and aluminum (25%).

[76] Women in International Trade (WIIT) event. The Value of Attending a World Trade Organization Ministerial Conference, January 20, 2006.

[77] "Sen. Grassley Warns Brazil, India, on GSP; Stops Short of Predicting Graduation," *Inside U.S. Trade*, May 19, 2006. "Thomas Urges USTR to Shift from Lagging Doha Round to Completing FTAs." Inside U.S. Trade, April 7, 2006.

[78] Washington International Trade Association (WITA) event. "The 2006 Congressional Trade Agenda," February 15, 2006.

[79] "Rangel Bill Would Extend Trade Benefits for Developing Countries," Press Release, March 30, 2006.

[80] While overall multilateral preferences may be eroding, the tariff benefits for individual items is still quite significant. For example, the U.S. tariff on flashlights (eligible for duty-free access for all BDCs) is 12.5% *ad valorem*. Some GSPeligible jewelry items have tariffs as high as 13.5%.

[81] Organization for International Cooperation and Development. *Market Access for the Least-Developed Countries: Where are the Obstacles?* Published by World Trade Organization, WT/LDC/HL/19, October 21, 1997, Table 12, p. 47. The study estimated that in 1997, the loss in the Canadian market was approximately 71%, in the EU 26%, in Japan 34%, and in the United States, 50% (hereinafter OECD study).

[82] Sanchez Arnau, Juan C. *The Generalized System of Preferences and the World Trade Organization*. London: Cameron May, Ltd., 2002, p. 282.

[83] Alliance to End Hunger, et al. Letter to House Ways and Means and Senate Finance Chairs and Ranking Members, April 22, 2009.

[84] Baldwin, R.E. and Murray, T. "MFN Tariff Reductions and Developing Country Trade Benefits Under the GSP," *Economic Journal* 87:345, March 1977, p. 46.

[85] OECD study, p. 27.

[86] 2008 GAO Report, pp.33-35.

[87] September 21, 2006 DC Bar meeting.

[88] Letter to United States Trade Representative Ron Kirk on renewal of trade preferences, signed by representatives of the Alliance to End Hunger, the American Apparel and Footwear Association, the Business Roundtable, and other business groups and NGOs, April 22, 2009.

[89] Ibid.

[90] Ibid.

[91] The Coalition for GSP. *The U.S. Generalized System of Preferences Program: An Integral Part of the U.S. Economy*. January 1997, p. 3.

[92] September 6, 2006 public comment letter to USTR from ActionAid International USA.

[93] "Grassley Throws Up Obstacle to Trade-Preference Renewal." *Congress Daily*, September 18, 2006.

[94] United States Government Accountability Office. *U.S. Trade Preference Programs: An Overview of Use by Beneficiaries and U.S. Administrative Reviews*. GAO-07-1209, September 2007, p. 4.

[95] "U.S. Retailers, Importers Push for GSP Renewal Despite Opposition," *Inside U.S. Trade*, May 5, 2006.

[96] Discussion with officials of the Joint Industry Group, August 18, 2006.

[97] 19 U.S.C. § 2463(c).

[98] "Administration Decides to Keep Russian GSP Benefits for Titanium," *Inside U.S. Trade,* July 9, 2004.

[99] 19 U.S.C. § 2466b, as amended by section 7 of the AGOA Acceleration Act of 2004 (P.L. 108-274).

[100] 19 U.S.C. § 2465.

[101] "Thomas Urges USTR to Shift from Lagging Doha Round Completing FTAs," *Inside U.S. Trade*, April 7, 2006.

[102] U.S. Senate, Committee on Foreign Relations. "Examining the Theft of American Intellectual Property at Home and Abroad." Hearing, February 12, 2002, S. Hrg. 107-457.

[103] 15 C.F.R. 2007.0(b).

[104] Vamvakidis, Ahtanasios. "Regional Trade Agreements or Broad Liberalization: Which Path Leads to Faster Growth?" *IMF Staff Papers*, Vol. 46:1, March 1999, p. 42.

[105] Haiti was recently provided additional preference benefits through the Haiti Economic Lift Act of 2010 (P.L. 111-171). See CRS Report RL34687, *The Haitian Economy and the HOPE Act*, by J. F. Hornbeck

[106] 19 U.S.C. § 2463(a)(2)(A)(ii)(II). The statute further specifies that a product may be made in one BDC or any two or more such countries that are members of the same association of countries and are treated as one under section 19 U.S.C. § 2467(2). For beneficiary countries under AGOA, this percentage may also include up to 15% (as to value) of U.S. origin (19 U.S.C. § 2466a(b)(2)).

[107] 19 U.S.C. § 2463(c).

[108] GAO Report, p. 55.

In: U.S. Trade Preferences…
Editor: Jonathan R. Ferreira

ISBN: 978-1-61324-378-7

Chapter 4

GENERALIZED SYSTEM OF PREFERENCES: AGRICULTURAL IMPORTS*

Renée Johnson

SUMMARY

The Generalized System of Preferences (GSP) provides duty-free tariff treatment for certain products from designated developing countries. Agricultural imports under the GSP totaled $2.2 billion in 2009, about 11% of all U.S. GSP imports. Leading agricultural imports include processed foods and food processing inputs, sugar and sugar confectionery, cocoa, processed and fresh fruits and vegetables, beverages and drinking waters, olive oil, processed meats, and miscellaneous food preparations and inputs for further processing. The majority of these imports are from Thailand, Brazil, Argentina, India, and the Philippines. Some in Congress have continued to call for changes to the program that could limit GSP benefits to certain countries, among other changes. Opinion within the U.S. agriculture industry is mixed, reflecting both support for and opposition to the current program. Congress made changes to the program in 2006, tightening its requirements on imports under certain circumstances.

In the past few years, Congress has extended GSP through a series of short-term extensions. However, the 111th Congress did not extend the GSP in 2010, and it was set to expire December 31, 2010 (P.L. 111-124).

* This is an edited, reformatted and augmented version of a Congressional Research Services publication, CRS Report for Congress RS22541, from www.crs.gov, dated January 3, 2011.

The expiration of the GSP will likely become a legislative issue in the 112th Congress. In addition, leaders of the House Ways and Means Committee and the Senate Finance Committee have continued to express an interest in evaluating the effectiveness of U.S. trade preference programs, including the GSP, and broader reform of these programs might be possible.

BACKGROUND

The U.S. Generalized System of Preferences (GSP) was established by the Trade Act of 1974 (19 U.S.C. 2465; Sec. 505) and now provides preferential duty-free entry to more than 4,800 agricultural and non-agricultural products from 131 designated beneficiary countries and territories.[1] Agricultural products under the GSP totaled $2.2 billion in 2009, accounting for about 11% of the total value of annual GSP imports. Duty-free access for agricultural imports under the program is an important issue for many in the U.S. agriculture industry who either support or oppose the program. However, some in Congress have called for changes to the program that could limit or curtail benefits to certain countries, among other changes. In 2008 and again in 2009, GSP was reauthorized through a series of one-year extensions. The 111th Congress did not extend the GSP in 2010, and it was set to expire December 31, 2010 (P.L. 111-124).[2]

GSP AGRICULTURAL IMPORTS

In 2008, U.S. imports under the GSP program totaled $20.3 billion, accounting for less than 2% of all commodity imports. Leading U.S. imports under the GSP are manufactured products and parts, chemicals, plastics, minerals, and forestry products. Roughly one-fourth of all GSP imports consist of jewelry, electrical, and transportation equipment, both finished products and parts.[3]

Agricultural products accounted for 11% of all imports under the GSP, totaling $2.2 billion in 2009. Compared to 2000, the value of agricultural imports under the program has nearly doubled. In 2009, imports under the GSP accounted for about 3% of total U.S. agricultural imports.[4] *Table 1* shows the leading agricultural products (ranked by value) imported into the United States under the GSP program. Leading imports include processed foods and food processing inputs, sugar and sugar confectionery, cocoa, processed and fresh fruits and vegetables, drinking waters, olive oil, processed meats, and miscellaneous food preparations and inputs for further processing.

Table 1. U.S. Agricultural Imports under GSP, 2009

HTS Chapter(s) Subsection	Import Categories	2009 ($ millions)	% Share	GSP Share All Ag Imports
19, 21, 13	Processed foods & food processing inputs	385.1	18%	5%
17	Sugar and sugar confectionary	378.9	17%	13%
20, 14	Processed fruits & vegetables, inputs	329.8	15%	7%
22	Beverages, water, spirits, and vinegar	152.7	7%	1%
1509	Olive oil	150.5	7%	17%
23, 3501-3505, 3301, 38 (part)	Other ag-based chemicals, residues, & byproducts	148.2	7%	3%
16	Processed meat & fish products	120.9	6%	3%
8 (part), 7	Other fresh fruits and vegetables	116.3	5%	1%
18	Cocoa & cocoa-containing products	102.1	5%	3%
8 (part)	Fresh tropical fruits	48.3	2%	2%
10, 11	Grain-based products	42.3	2%	1%
12, 15 (part)	Oilseeds & processed oils/fats	41.3	2%	1%
24	Tobacco products	39.5	2%	3%
4	Dairy products	36.8	2%	2%
9	Coffee, tea, & spices	33.2	2%	1%
2905 (part)	Ag-based organic chemicals (e.g. sorbitol)	19.7	1%	25%
6	Plants and cut flowers	15.8	1%	3%
5, 4301, 41 (part)	Misc. animal products, incl. hides	5.3	0%	1%
8 (part)	Nuts	3.6	0%	0%
1, 2	Meat products, incl. live animals	0.3	0%	0%
50-53 (part)	Ag-based textile inputs (cotton, wool)	0.2	0%	0%
	Total	2,170.8	100%	3%

Source: CRS calculations from data from U.S. International Trade Commission, http://dataweb.usitc.gov. Imports for consumption, actual U.S. dollars. Select GSP countries ranked by value of imports. Agriculture commodities as defined by the WTO Agreement on Agriculture. Includes U.S. Harmonized Tariff Schedule chapters 1-24, excluding chapter 3 (fish and fish products, except processed), and parts of chapters 29, 33, 35, 48, 41, 43, and 50-53 (USDA, *Profiles of Tariffs in Global Agricultural Markets*, AER-796, Appendix, January 2001).

Most GSP agricultural imports are supplied by beneficiary countries that have been identified for possible graduation from the program. In 2009, the top six beneficiary countries ranked by import value—Thailand, Brazil, Argentina, India, the Philippines, and Turkey—accounted for the majority of agricultural imports under the GSP (see *Table 2*). Brazil and India accounted for nearly one-fifth of agricultural imports under the program. These countries are among those identified by critics of GSP as countries whose benefits under the program should be limited or curtailed.

More than 20% of GSP agricultural imports consist of sugar and sugar-based products, and cocoa and cocoa-containing products. Sugar and confectionery imports accounted for 18% of the value of agricultural imports under the GSP program (*Table 1*). Major GSP suppliers of cane and beet sugar imports were the Philippines, Paraguay, Peru, Panama, and South Africa. Major suppliers of confectionery were Brazil, Argentina, Colombia, the Philippines, South Africa, Thailand, and Turkey. Cocoa and cocoa-containing products accounted for 5% of GSP agricultural imports, and were supplied mainly by Brazil, the Côte d'Ivoire, and other African nations. Indonesia, among other countries, is a supplier of imports of sugar alcohols and other agriculture-based organic chemicals, such as sorbitol.

Table 2. U.S. Agricultural Imports under GSP, by Country, 2009

Country of Origin	2009 ($ millions)	% Share	% Change 2005-2009	Major import product categories
Thailand	425.4	19.6%	48%	food preparations, preserved fruits and vegetables, waters, grain products, sauces and condiments, confectionery,
Brazil	273.0	12.6%	30%	fruit juices, gelatin derivatives, sugar confectionery, tropical fruits, miscellaneous food preparations, cocoa products
Argentina	241.7	11.1%	24%	casein, olive oil, prepared meats, gelatin derivatives, cheese and curd, sugar confectionery, wine
India	211.9	9.8%	71%	vegetable saps/extracts, gelatin derivatives, preserved cucumbers, essential oils (peppermint), spices
Philippines	137.1	6.3%	18%	cane/beet sugar, fresh/processed fruits and tropical fruits, fish products, coconut oil and coconuts, grains, waters

Country of Origin	2009 ($ millions)	% Share	% Change 2005-2009	Major import product categories
Turkey	131.7	6.1%	16%	sugar confectionary, olive oil, prepared/preserved fruits and vegetables, fruit juices, condiments and spices
Tunisia	106.1	4.9%	406%	olive oil and olive products, tropical fruits, sugar confectionary, sauces and condiments, spices
Indonesia	78.9	3.6%	61%	sugar alcohols and organic chemicals, seafood, tobacco products, sugar confectionary, edible animal products
Colombia	72.6	3.3%	1%	sugar and confectionary, miscellaneous food preparations, molasses, tropical fruits/vegetables, cocoa products
Fiji	47.4	2.2%	-20%	mineral waters, molasses, tropical fruits/vegetables, grain products, miscellaneous food preparations, plants
South Africa	42.1	1.9%	34%	sugar, wine, fish products, yeasts, live plants and seeds, essential oils, food preparations, spices
Cote d`Ivoire	40.8	1.9%	85%	preserved/frozen fruit products, sugar, floriculture/plants, seeds, bulbs, tuber vegetables
Pakistan	34.9	1.6%	272%	cane/beet sugar, rice, miscellaneous food preparations, spices, fresh/processed fruits and tropical fruits
Ecuador	33.4	1.5%	52%	tropical fruits/vegetables, prepared fish products, miscellaneous food preparations, fruit juices, cocoa products
Venezuela	29.2	1.3%	161%	
Subtotal	1,906	87.8%	42%	
Other	265	12.2%	16%	
Total	2,171	100.0%	-49%	

Source: CRS calculations from data from U.S. International Trade Commission (USITC),

http://dataweb.usitc.gov. Imports for consumption, actual U.S. dollars. Includes U.S. Harmonized Tariff Schedule (HTS) chapters 1-24, excluding chapter 3 (fish and fish products, except processed), and parts of HTS chapters 29, 33, 35, 48, 41, 43, and 50-53. Select GSP countries ranked in terms of value of imports in 2007 (10-digit HTS level). Agriculture commodities as defined by the WTO Agreement on Agriculture (for information, see USDA, *Profiles of Tariffs in Global Agricultural Markets*, AER-796, Appendix, January 2001).

Another nearly 40% of agricultural imports under the GSP program include food processing inputs, such as miscellaneous processed foods, processed oils and fats, fruit and vegetable preparations, and ag-based chemicals and byproducts. Other product categories and suppliers are as follows. Olive oil accounted for 7% of GSP agricultural imports in 2009, supplied by Tunisia, Turkey, and Argentina. Mineral waters and other types of nonalcoholic beverages (another 6%) were supplied by Fiji and Thailand, among others. Imports of fresh and prepared fruits and vegetables (about 10%) include bananas and other tropical produce.

LEGISLATIVE AND ADMINISTRATIVE CHANGES TO GSP

In the past few years, Congress has extended GSP through a series of short-term extensions. However, the 111th Congress did not extend the GSP in 2010, and it was set to expire December 31, 2010 (P.L. 111-124). The expiration of the GSP will likely become a legislative issue in the 112th Congress, especially since many in Congress continue to support the program.[5] In addition, the leaders of the House Ways and Means Committee and the Senate Finance Committee have continued to express an interest in evaluating the effectiveness of U.S. trade preference programs, including the GSP, and broader reform of these programs has been expected in recent years.

The House Ways and Means Subcommittee on Trade conducted a hearing evaluating the effectiveness of U.S. trade preference programs, including the GSP, in November 2009;[6] the Senate Finance Committee conducted an oversight hearing in June 2008, focusing on ways to reform U.S. trade preference programs.[7] Prior to the one-year extension in December 2009, the Obama Administration had indicated that the debate on preference reform may extend into next year; however, some Members have expressed their reluctance to pass a GSP renewal without also enacting meaningful reform legislation.[8]

Amendments to the GSP in 2006 followed extensive debate about the program during the 109th Congress. Specifically, some in Congress questioned the inclusion of certain more advanced developing countries (BDCs)[9] as beneficiaries under the GSP and also commented that certain BDCs had contributed to the ongoing impasse in multilateral trade talks in the WTO Doha Development Agenda.[10] In response to these concerns, Congress amended the program in 2006 by tightening the rules on "competitive need limits" (CNL)[11] waivers that allow imports from beneficiary countries in excess of GSP statutory thresholds for some products (P.L. 109-432).

Historically, there have been few CNL waivers to the GSP for agricultural products and it is unlikely that these program changes will greatly affect U.S. agricultural imports under the program. In 2006, Congress had also renewed the GSP for two years through 2008.

Also, in 2006, the Trade Policy Staff Committee (TPSC), an advisory committee chaired by the U.S. Trade Representative, instituted a series of investigations to evaluate possible changes to the GSP.[12] In its 2006 review the TPSC announced that the more than 80 previously granted CNL waivers would be individually evaluated, in addition to the standard practice of examining petitions for new CNL waivers. The TPSC said that it would also examine the eligibility status of several "middle income" economies.[13] Among the countries identified for possible removal as beneficiaries under the program were Argentina, Brazil, India, the Philippines, Thailand, and Turkey. These countries account for over 60% of the value of U.S. agricultural products imported duty-free under the program. Although none of the countries cited lost their overall GSP eligibility as a result of these reviews, several previously granted CNL waivers from these countries were revoked. For agricultural imports under the GSP, the Côte d'Ivoire lost CNL waivers for fresh or dried, shelled kola nuts (HTS 0802.90.94), as part of the 2006 review. Argentina lost CNL waivers for cooked, shelled, fresh or dried peanuts (HTS 1202.20.40), as part of the 2007 review. These waivers had allowed for these products to be imported from the Côte d'Ivoire and Argentina duty-free under GSP despite the statutory import thresholds. Other countries lost CNL waivers for some non-agricultural products, but not for agricultural products. The 2006 review included decisions on other country and product petitions involving agricultural products, but these changes are unlikely to greatly affect U.S. agricultural imports under the GSP.

POSSIBLE IMPLICATIONS OF CHANGES TO THE GSP

The 2006 statutory changes to the GSP tightening rules for CNL waivers are unlikely to greatly affect U.S. agricultural imports under the program. Historically, there have been few CNL waivers for agricultural products imported duty-free under the GSP. Current waivers include sugar and preserved bananas (Philippines), sugar, carnations, figs, yams, and gelatin derivatives (Colombia), certain nuts (Argentina), animal hides (Argentina,

South Africa, and Thailand), and caviar (Russia). Other types of program changes, however, could affect U.S. agricultural imports under the GSP, including additional limits on CNL waivers from certain countries or graduation of some beneficiary countries. Countries that account for the majority of U.S. agricultural imports under the GSP are Thailand, Brazil, Argentina, India, the Philippines, and Turkey.

Comments submitted to USTR as part of its 2006 review from U.S. agricultural industry groups are mixed.[14] For example, the American Farm Bureau Federation (AFBF) expressed its generalopposition to the GSP program, stating that products imported duty-free under the program compete with U.S.-produced goods without granting a commensurate level of opportunity for U.S. producers in foreign markets. AFBF further supported withdrawal of CNL waivers for the Philippines, Argentina, and Colombia. The Grocery Manufacturers Association (GMA) expressed support for the current GSP program and identified certain agricultural products of importance to GMA under the program, including sugar confections, spices, and certain processed foods and inputs from Brazil, India, and Argentina. GMA's position was generally supported by comments from the American Spice Trade Association, the National Confectioners Association, and the Chocolate Manufacturers Association. GMA also was a signatory of a letter sent to House and Senate leaders in late 2010 urging Congress to extend the GSP.[15]

What remains unclear is whether duty-free access for most agricultural imports under the GSP greatly influences a country's willingness to export these products to the United States. In most cases, costs associated with import tariffs are borne by the importer. These costs may be passed on to the BDCs in terms of lower import prices. However, import tariffs to the United States for most of these products tend to be low. As calculated by CRS, *ad valorem* equivalent tariffs range from 3%-4% for sugar, 2%-10% for cocoa-containing products, 5%-12% for confectionery, 1%- 2% for most processed meats, about 2% for olive oil, less than 1% for mineral water, and about 5% for agriculture-based organic chemicals.[16] In general, any additional costs that might be incurred by the BDCs as a result of the proposed changes could be more than offset by the generally higher U.S. prices for most products compared to prices in other world markets. Nevertheless, the imposition of even relatively low import tariffs could represent an increase in input costs to some U.S. food processors and industrial users. These costs could be passed on to consumers through higher prices for these and other finished agricultural or manufactured products. As shown in Table 1, about one-half of GSP agricultural imports are intermediate goods and inputs, such as raw sugar, miscellaneous processed foods, preparations, and byproducts, and agriculture-based organic chemicals.

End Notes

[1] Office of the U.S. Trade Representative (USTR), Generalized System of Preferences, http://www.ustr.gov/ Trade_Development/Preference_Programs/GSP/Section_Index.html.

[2] The African Growth and Opportunity Acceleration Act of 2004 (P.L. 108-274) extended GSP preferences for all beneficiary developing sub-Saharan African countries under the African Growth and Opportunity Act through September 30, 2015.

[3] U.S. Chamber of Commerce, *Estimated Impacts of the U.S. Generalized System of Preferences to U.S. Industry and Consumers*, October, 2006, http://www.uschamber.com/reports/ estimated-impacts-us-generalized-system-preferencesus-industry

[4] The value of U.S. agricultural imports totaled $78.8 billion in 2009 (compiled by CRS using trade data from U.S. International Trade Commission. Imports for consumption, actual U.S. dollars. Agriculture commodities as defined by the WTO Agreement on Agriculture (USDA, *Profiles of Tariffs in Global Agricultural Markets*, AER-796, Appendix, January 2001).

[5] "Congress Passes Short-Term ATPDEA, TAA Extensions, But Not GSP," *Inside U.S. Trade*, December 23, 2010; and press release of Senator Max Baucus, "Baucus Commends Passage of Short-Term Extension of Job-Creating Trade Bill, Seeks Longer Extension," December 22, 2010.

[6] House Ways and Means Subcommittee on Trade, "Hearing on the Operation, Impact, and Future of the U.S. Preference Programs," November 17, 2009.

[7] Senate Finance Committee, "Oversight of Trade Functions: Customs and Other Trade Agencies," June 24, 2008.

[8] See, e.g., remarks of Senator Charles Grassley, Ranking Member of Senate Finance Committee, Washington International Trade Association, June 18, 2009.

[9] A current listing of BDCs under the GSP is available in the U.S. Harmonized Tariff Schedule (General Notes).

[10] See, e.g., U.S. Senate, Committee on Finance, Opening Statement of Senator Charles Grassley, Hearing on the Nomination of Susan C. Schwab to be U.S. Trade Representative, May 16, 2006.

[11] The previous law stipulated a CNL requiring that countries export no more than 50% of total U.S. imports of each product or no more than a specified dollar amount of the imports for a given year. The amended law further tightened these requirements.

[12] 72 *Federal Register* 35895, June 28, 2007 (2006 Review); and 73 *Federal Register* 38297, June 3, 2008 (2007 Review). Regulations for implementing the GSP are at 15 C.F.R. Part 2007.

[13] Countries may "graduate" or be removed as a beneficiary developing country if the country is determined to be sufficiently competitive or developed (19 U.S.C. 2462(e)). For example, in 2008, the Republic of Trinidad and Tobago graduated from the GSP program when it was determined to have become a "high income" country. Also, countries that formally enter into a bilateral trading relationship with another developed country may also become ineligible, as happened in 2007 for Bulgaria and Romania when they joined the European Union.

[14] Based on public comments to the 2006 TPSC recommendations, posted at USTR's website.

[15] Letter to Representatives Sander Levin and Dave Camp, and Senators Max Baucus and Charles Grassley, from several U.S. companies and manufacturing associations, including GMA, November 10, 2010, https://www.apparelandfootwear.org/UserFiles/File/Letters/2010/111010gspcoalition.pdf.

[16] Calculated tariffs based on the in-quota rate. Under the GSP, agricultural products subject to a TRQ exceeding the in-quota quantity is ineligible for duty-free import (19 U.S.C. 2463(b)(3)).

In: U.S. Trade Preferences…
Editor: Jonathan R. Ferreira

ISBN: 978-1-61324-378-7

Chapter 5

POTENTIAL TRADE EFFECTS OF ADDING VIETNAM TO THE GENERALIZED SYSTEM OF PREFERENCES PROGRAM*

Michael F. Martin and Vivian C. Jones

SUMMARY

In May 2008, Vietnam formally requested to be added to the U.S. Generalized System of Preferences (GSP) program as a "developing country." On June 20, 2008, the office of the U.S. Trade Representative (USTR) announced that it was initiating a formal review of Vietnam's eligibility for GSP benefits and would accept public comments on the application until August 4, 2008. Vietnam has already been accepted into several other developed-country GSP programs around the world, including Canada, the European Union (EU), and Japan.

The GSP statute provides the President with the authority to designate any country a beneficiary developing country, provided the country complies with various trade and investment policies and labor conditions. Congress does not need to act to approve GSP status for Vietnam. The President is, however, required to notify Congress of his intention. The inclusion of Vietnam into the GSP program is generally viewed as another step in the development of closer bilateral relations.

* A version of this chapter was also published in *Vietnam and its Relations with the U.S.*, edited by Edward C. Mason published by Nova Science Publishers, Inc. It was submitted for appropriate modifications in an effort to encourage wider dissemination of research.

Most of the public comments submitted to the USTR were supportive of approving Vietnam's application. However, there were some issues raised that could cause problems in accepting Vietnam into the GSP program—in particular, Vietnam's record on workers' rights. In addition, Vietnam's record on human rights may also have an impact on its application, even though the President is not legally required to consider this issue when evaluating Vietnam's application.

If accepted into the GSP program, up to 3,400 different types of exports from Vietnam could potentially enter into the United States duty-free. While Vietnam's leading exports to the United States—knitted and non-knitted clothing—are deemed "import sensitive" and therefore excluded from GSP eligibility, some of its fastest growing exports are eligible for duty-free status under the GSP. These exports include electrical machinery, fruits, and coffee preparations. Imports of these commodities would likely increase if Vietnam is granted beneficiary developing country (BDC) status. This could lead to an increase in the U.S. bilateral trade deficit with Vietnam and a shift in the mix of U.S. imports from Vietnam. It might also foster a relocation of some assembly operations from China to Vietnam, thereby reducing the U.S. bilateral trade deficit with China.

A one-year extension of the Generalized System of Preferences program was included in H.R. 7222, which was passed in the House (September 29, 2008 and October 3, 2008) and Senate (October 2, 2008), and became P.L. 110-436 on October 16, 2008.

INTRODUCTION

In May 2008, the Socialist Republic of Vietnam (Vietnam) formally requested consideration for designation as a "beneficiary developing country" (BDC) under the United States' Generalized System of Preferences (GSP) program. If accepted into the GSP program, up to 3,400 different types of exports from Vietnam could potentially enter into the United States dutyfree. While Vietnam's top export to the United States—clothing—is not GSP-eligible, other leading exports, such as electrical machinery, fruits, and coffee preparations, could benefit from Vietnam's addition to the GSP program. Vietnam has already been accepted into several other developed-country GSP programs around the world, including Canada, the European Union (EU), and Japan.

On June 20, 2008, the U.S. Trade Representative (USTR) announced that it was initiating a review of Vietnam's eligibility for GSP benefits, and solicited comments on the matter until August 4, 2008.[1] Five days later, Vietnam's Prime Minister Nguyen Tan Dung raised the issue of Vietnam's GSP application with then President Bush during his official visit to the White House. In a joint statement issued after their meeting, "President Bush affirmed that the United States is seriously reviewing Vietnam's request to be designated as a beneficiary of the Generalized System of Preferences program."[2] To date, no decision has been made on Vietnam's GSP application.

Vietnam's addition to the U.S. GSP program is generally viewed as another step in the process of promoting the continued growth of trade relations and expanding bilateral ties between the two countries. In December 2006, Congress passed and President Bush signed H.R. 6111 (P.L. 109-432), extending permanent normal trade relations (PNTR) status to Vietnam. On January 11, 2007, Vietnam acceded into membership in the World Trade Organization (WTO). On June 21, 2007, the two nations concluded a Trade and Investment Framework Agreement (TIFA).[3] During their summit meeting (the fourth such meeting in four years), Prime Minister Dung and President Bush also discussed initiating negotiations of a Bilateral Investment Treaty (BIT). Vietnam has also expressed an interest in eventually negotiating a Free Trade Agreement (FTA) with the United States.

WHAT IS GSP?

The Generalized System of Preferences (GSP) provides non-reciprocal preferential tariff treatment to certain products imported from designated developing countries. The United States, the European Union, and other developed countries implemented such programs in the 1970s in order to promote economic growth in developing countries by stimulating their exports. The U.S. program was established by Title V of the Trade Act of 1974 (P.L. 93-618) for a 10-year period. Since then, Congress has extended the program nine times, most recently through December 31, 2008, in section 8002 of P.L. 109-432.4 The House and Senate recently passed a one-year extension of GSP in section 4 of H.R. 7222, which became P.L. 110-436 on October 16, 2008.

The basic principle behind the GSP is to provide certain goods originating in developing countries with preferential market access (usually in the form of lower tariff rates or duty-free status) to developed country markets in order to spur economic growth. The program was first adopted internationally in 1968 by the United Nations Conference on Trade and Development (UNCTAD) at the UNCTAD II Conference.

In general, the U.S. GSP program authorizes the President to grant duty-free treatment under the GSP for any eligible product from any beneficiary developing country (BDC) or least-developed beneficiary developing country (LDBDC). The statute also provides the President with specific political and economic criteria to use when designating eligible countries and products.[5]

Country Eligibility

Under the GSP eligibility criteria, there are certain mandatory factors that may not be waived. First, certain developed countries are specifically excluded.[6] Other mandatory criteria require exclusion of any country that:

- is "Communist," *unless* it has normal trade relation status with the United States; is a member in the World Trade Organization (WTO) and the International Monetary Fund (IMF); and it is "not dominated or controlled by international communism";
- engages in actions that would restrict or raise prices of vital commodities;
- provides trade preferences to developed countries other than the United States which has, or is likely to have, a significant adverse effect on United States commerce.

Other mandatory criteria may be waived "if the President determines that such designation will be in the national economic interest of the United States and reports such determination to the Congress with the reasons therefor." These criteria preclude countries that:

- have nationalized or expropriated the property of U.S. citizens or companies;
- have failed to acknowledge or enforce arbitral awards that are in U.S. favor;
- aided or abetted individuals or groups that have engaged in international terrorism;
- have not taken steps to provide its workers with internationally recognized worker rights; or
- have not taken steps to "eliminate the worst forms of child labor."[7]

Other discretionary factors that the President may consider when deciding to confer BDC status are: (1) the desire of the country to be designated; (2) the level of economic development of the country, including gross national product (GNP) and living standards; (3) whether other developed countries offer similar tariff benefits to the country; (4) the degree to which the country has agreed to provide equitable and reasonable access to its markets, commodities, and resources; (5) the level of protection it provides to intellectual property; (6) the extent to which it has reduced barriers to trade and investment; and (7) the degree to which it has provided its workers with workers rights including collective bargaining, a minimum age for child labor, and prohibition of forced labor or the worst forms of child labor.[8]

PRODUCT ELIGIBILITY

The President is authorized to designate products as eligible for GSP treatment after consultation with the International Trade Commission.[9] Products are designated generally for all GSP recipients to the extent that countries have not exceeded statutory limits for importing certain products. Product eligibility under GSP is also restricted in the law by several factors. First, the GSP statute specifically excludes certain categories of goods as "import-sensitive," including textiles and apparel; certain watches; footwear and other accessories; certain electronics, steel, and glass products; and certain agricultural products subject to tariff-rate quotas.[10]

Second, the law establishes automatic "competitive need limits" (CNLs) that require the President to suspend GSP treatment if imports of a product from a single country reach a specified threshold value ($135 million in 2008) or if 50% or more of total U.S. imports of a product entering under GSP come from a single country (unless a waiver is granted).[11] Third, GSP rules of origin only allow duty-free entry if the article is imported directly from the beneficiary country, and at least 35% of the value (of materials and/or processing) of an eligible product is the "growth, product, or manufacture" of a beneficiary developing country.[12]

Process for Vietnam

An evaluation of Vietnam's eligibility for GSP status began with a Federal Register notice announcing the review.[13] Public comments were solicited from

June 20, 2008 to August 4, 2008.[14] A subsequent review to determine whether Vietnam complies with the statutory requirements for designation as a GSP beneficiary will be administered by the GSP Subcommittee of the Trade Policy Staff Committee (TPSC), an interagency group chaired by the USTR.[15] The USTR may also, as necessary, request that the International Trade Commission evaluate the potential trade effects of Vietnam's GSP request.[16] At the conclusion of the review, the TPSC will present its findings to the USTR, who will, in turn, present a recommendation to the President. The final decision to grant Vietnam GSP eligibility or not will be made by the President.

Evaluating Vietnam's Prospects

Vietnam's acceptance into the U.S. GSP program will hinge on a combination of the TPSC's evaluation (and the President's subsequent approval) of Vietnam's compliance with these eligibility criteria, and the perceived acceptability of including Vietnam as a beneficiary developing country.

Compliance with Eligibility Criteria

There may be some ambiguity regarding Vietnam's compliance with both the mandatory and discretionary GSP criteria. For the four mandatory criteria, the most debatable issue may be its classification as a "Communist country," and more specifically whether or not it is controlled or dominated by "international communism." Among the criteria that may be waived or assessed on a more progressive basis, the most likely source of challenges is Vietnam's record in providing workers with internationally recognized workers' rights.

Is Vietnam a "Communist Country"?

U.S. federal law does not currently include a specific definition of what constitutes a "Communist country." The concept of Communism has two distinct common definitions—one political and one economic. The political definition typically hinges on the domination of society's political system by a single and self-perpetuating party. The economic definition is usually based on the holding of all property in common, with the ownership being ascribed to the community as a whole or to the state.

Politically, the Vietnamese government does not refer to itself as communist country, but as socialist republic. However, Vietnam is a one-party state controlled by the Communist Party of Vietnam (VCP). Since the mid-1990s, the VCP appears to have followed a strategy of permitting most forms of personal and religious expression while selectively repressing individuals and organizations that it deems a threat to the party's monopoly on power.

Economically, Vietnam has been steadily transforming its centrally planned economy into a market economy, and has allowed the creation and growth of private enterprise. Vietnam's constitution and civil code recognize and protect private property rights. Yet, government influence and control over Vietnam's economy still remains comparatively high.[17]

Even if Vietnam were determined to be a "Communist country," GSP statutory provisions specify that it can still qualify for GSP status if it is a member of the WTO and IMF, received NTR status from the United States, and is found to be "not dominated or controlled by international communism." Vietnam is a recent member of the WTO (date of accession January 11, 2007) and a member of long-standing in the IMF (since September 1956). In December 2006, Vietnam was conferred permanent NTR status by the United States. In addition, given that the Soviet Union and its Council for Mutual Economic Assistance (Comecon) no longer exist, it is unclear how to define what constitutes "domination or control by international communism."

Workers' Rights

Among the five mandatory, but discretionary, criteria, Vietnam's recognition of internationally-accepted workers' rights may prove to be the most controversial. Prior to the 1986 advent of *doi moi*, Vietnam's process of market-oriented economic renovation, there were many allegations about substandard working conditions in Vietnam, including "sweatshop" working conditions, the use of child labor, and severe restrictions on the right of association and collective bargaining.[18] Since then, the Vietnamese government is generally perceived to have made concerted efforts to comply with internationally-recognized labor standards.

In its statement of support for GSP designation, the Vietnamese government focused on its partnership with the International Labor Organization (ILO) and its ratification of several of the ILO's conventions as demonstrating its commitment to comply with international labor rights standards. Vietnam rejoined the ILO as a member state in 1992 and has worked with the ILO in drafting new labor laws, including the 1994 Labor Code. In addition, Vietnam has ratified five of the eight fundamental ILO conventions—covering compulsory labor, income inequality, discrimination, minimum age, and the worst forms of child labor—and an additional 12 other ILO conventions. Vietnam reported it is considering ratification of two more conventions, concerning the freedom of association and the right to collective bargaining. In addition, the United States and Vietnam signed a Memorandum of Understanding regarding labor cooperation in November 2000, which has fostered the exchange in technical expertise and training on a broad range of labor issues.

Freedom of Association

Despite the aforementioned efforts by the Vietnamese government, critics still maintain that working conditions remain below international standards. In particular, Vietnam has been criticized for its failure to allow independent labor unions and respect the right of association. At present, all labor unions in Vietnam must be a member of the Vietnam General Confederation of Labor (VGCL). Efforts to organize independent unions in Vietnam reportedly have been thwarted by government suppression, including the arrest and imprisonment of union leaders. In Vietnam's GSP submission, the government maintains that "the Vietnam Constitution of 1992, along with other domestic laws, guarantees that workers have the right of association" and that "citizens are entitled to freedom of speech and freedom of the press; they have the right to receive information and the right of assembly, association and demonstration in accordance with the law."[19]

Despite the provisions in Vietnam's constitution, some observers maintain that the ability of workers to form independent unions has, to some extent, been thwarted. According to Amnesty International, two days after Tran Quoc Hien was chosen as spokesperson for the United Workers-Farmers Organization (UWFO) in January 2007, he was arrested. The Vietnamese authorities claimed that he and his accomplices incited demonstrations and posted "distorted" articles on the Internet. On May 15, 2007, Tran Quoc Hien was sentenced to five years' imprisonment plus two years' probation.[20] Human Rights Watch also reports that some leaders of independent unions have been arrested, harassed and intimidated.[21]

Other observers conclude that since the launch of the *doi moi* reforms, worker rights have made progress despite the restrictions on the right to organize. In addition, hundreds of unaffiliated (and therefore unofficial) "labor associations" have sprouted without significant repression, and in many recent cases, Vietnamese workers went on strike reportedly because they felt that they were not well-represented by the official union.

Workers in Vietnam have the legal right to collective bargaining; the VGCL is supposed to organize a union within six months of the establishment of any new business, regardless of its ownership—state, foreign, or private. According to the State Department's 2008 *Country Report on Human Rights Practices*, "In actuality only 85 percent of state-owned enterprises, 60 percent of foreign-invested enterprises, and 30 percent of private enterprises were unionized."

Right to Strike

According to the government of Vietnam, strikes are not uncommon in Vietnam, and the Labor Code was amended in late 2006 in order to clarify the cases in which a strike may occur (i.e., after a legally mandated dispute resolution process has been carried out).[22] Vietnamese officials also maintain that there are many strikes in Vietnam, and that even in cases where strikes are deemed "illegal," the law prohibits retribution against strikers.[23]

Vietnam reports that there were 541 strikes in 2007 and 649 during the first eight months of 2008.[24] Many of these strikes arose spontaneously, without trade union leadership.[25] In most cases, the workers have struck for higher wages and better working conditions. Many of the strikes have occurred at foreign-owned enterprises, particularly at South Korean and Taiwanese manufacturing facilities.[26] The Vietnamese government—led by the Ministry of Labor, War Invalids and Social Affairs (MoLISA)—for the most part has not moved against the strikes, despite the fact that many have been technically illegal.

Action in Congress

Many in Congress continue to be concerned about Vietnam's human rights record. On October 1, 2008, Senator Barbara Boxer introduced S. 3678, the Vietnam Human Rights Act of 2008. Among other things, this bill seeks to prohibit the President from granting GSP benefits to Vietnam unless the President determines and certifies to Congress that the Government of Vietnam (1) fully protects the right of freedom of association in both law and practice; and (2) does not practice or condone serious violations of workers' rights, including detention, harassment, or arrest of labor activists or of individuals who write, speak, or otherwise disseminate information on labor rights.

Others in Congress see the granting of GSP status to Vietnam as an important foreign policy tool, much like the U.S. grant of PNTR status to Vietnam and U.S. support of its WTO accession. First, some see the value in continuing to expand relations with a country that continues to have an ambivalent relationship with China.[27] Second, many also believe that continued engagement with Vietnam in the commercial policy arena can serve as an indirect encouragement for the government to promote increased pluralism, accountability, and adherence to the "rule of law."[28] Some believe that continued normalization of relations with Vietnam is also symbolically important because it places greater distance between the U.S.-Vietnam relationship and the legacy of the Vietnam war.[29]

Public Comments on GSP Status for Vietnam

As part of the process of assessing Vietnam's suitability for the GSP program, the USTR accepted public comments until August 4, 2008. Over 20 different organizations and companies submitted comments. Eighteen of the commentators supported Vietnam's acceptance in the GSP program; two opposed it; and three expressed some reservations, but stopped short of stating their opposition.

Supporters of adding Vietnam as a BDC in the GSP program generally pointed to several factors. They maintained that it would be beneficial to both Vietnam and the United States economically and politically. In addition, it would help raise many of the people of Vietnam out of poverty— one of the principal goals of the GSP program. The supporters also pointed to Vietnam's *doi moi* policies as evidence of its compliance with the GSP eligibility and then indicated that acceptance into the GSP program would help progress Vietnam's transformation into a market economy. Some indicated that by including Vietnam in the GSP program, U.S. companies would have a feasible alternative to locating manufacturing facilities in China, which would improve their competitiveness in the global market and potentially reduce the U.S. trade deficit with China. Others cautioned that the exclusion of Vietnam from the GSP program might hinder the ability of U.S. companies to compete for investment opportunities in Vietnam.

Three commentators—the American Federation of Labor and Congress of Industrial Organizations (AFL-CIO), the International Intellectual Property Alliance (IIPA), and the Pharmaceutical Research and Manufacturers of America (PhRMA)—pointed out problems or issues with Vietnam's compliance with the GSP eligibility criteria, but did not directly state their opposition to adding Vietnam to the program. The AFL-CIO's criticisms focused on its assessment that "much more needs to be done to bring its [Vietnam's] labor laws and practices in line with internationally recognized worker rights."[30] In particular, the AFL-CIO cited continuing problems with Vietnamese workers' freedom of association, their right to organize and bargain collectively, restrictions on the ability to strike, and problems in working conditions (minimum wage enforcement, excessive working hours, and unsafe working conditions).

The IIPA's comments centered on Vietnam's compliance with the intellectual property rights (IPR) standards and market access requirements for GSP eligibility.[31] On IPR protection, the IIPA maintained that 90% of business software and 95% of records and music in Vietnam are pirate copies. In addition, the IIPA stated that Vietnam continues to restrict foreign access to its motion picture, home video, broadcast, and music/sound recording markets. Despite their apparent misgivings about Vietnam's GSP application, the IIPA suggests that it be granted one year of eligibility, with renewal subject to a review of Vietnam's progress on IPR protection.

The submission by PhRMA also focused on the issue of IPR protection in Vietnam, but with an emphasis on its application to pharmaceuticals.[32] Specific topics raised by PhRMA in its comments included IPR enforcement, data exclusivity, trademark infringement, counterfeiting, and "trade dress" violations.[33] PhRMA also expressed concern about market access and pricing restrictions in Vietnam's pharmaceuticals market.

There were two submissions to USTR—one by the U.S. Committee to Protect Vietnamese Workers (CPVW) and another by the U.S. producers of polyethylene carrier bags—that opposed GSP for Vietnam. The U.S. Committee to Protect Vietnamese Workers was established by a group of overseas Vietnamese "to protect the rights and interests of all Vietnamese workers."[34] In their comments to USTR, the CPVW indicated that it supported acceptance of Vietnam into the GSP program "in principle," but opposed the acceptance in practice because "Vietnam has not met even the basic GSP criteria on labor." The CPVW maintained that Vietnam failed to meet the eligibility criteria for the right of association, the right of assembly, the right to organize and bargain collectively, the prohibition of forced or compulsory labor, minimum age requirements and child labor, working conditions, and compensation requirements. The CPVW concluded their comments with a list of seven specific conditions to be met before granting GSP eligibility to Vietnam.

The comments in opposition by the U.S. producers of polyethylene carrier bags focused on the reputed damage to their industry from the recent rapid increase in plastic bag imports from China, Malaysia, and Thailand. According to their submission, antidumping duties on plastic bag imports from those three countries have slowed import growth, but have also led to a relocation of operations to Vietnam. Based on their reported experience, the U.S. producers requested that "Vietnam be precluded from seeking GSP treatment" for polyethylene carrier bags.

Human Rights in Vietnam

The human rights conditions in a country do not legally prevent the President from designating a country as eligible to receive GSP status. However, the issue of human rights in Vietnam has been an important factor in every previous case when the United States has considered strengthening bilateral trade relations.

It is difficult to make country-wide generalizations about the state of human rights in Vietnam. On the one hand, the VCP has permitted the growth of an independent press, so long as its criticism of the government is limited to issues such as corruption, economic policy, nature conservation and environmental pollution. Similarly, the Vietnamese government has generally allowed the freedom of worship, regardless of faith, so long as the religious organization registers with the authorities. As of 2006, Vietnam was no longer listed as a "country of particular concern" (CPC) in the State Department's *International Religious Freedom Report.*

On the other hand, the VCP regularly represses groups and individuals it perceives as a potential threat to its political power. Human Rights Watch claims that the Vietnamese government cracked down on democracy advocates during U.S. Deputy Secretary of State John Negroponte's September 2008 trip to Vietnam, detaining and interrogating "at least a dozen" activists.[35] Earlier in September, the Vietnamese government broke up a protest in Hanoi organized by Catholics who claim that a previously state-owned company (since privatized) had unlawfully been given land belonging to a Catholic church.[36] In July 2008, there were reported tensions between the Vietnamese government and the banned Unified Buddhist Church of Vietnam in making the funeral arrangements for their late patriarch, Thich Huyen Quang.[37]

POTENTIAL IMPACT ON U.S. TRADE

Projecting the impact of Vietnam becoming a BDC under the U.S. GSP program on its bilateral trade with the United States is difficult for a variety of technical reasons.[38] Scholarly studies of both the U.S. and EU GSP programs on developing countries' exports have come to differing conclusions. However, the rapid rise in bilateral trade following the U.S. extension of NTR to Vietnam may indicate that Vietnam's exports to the United States will increase if it becomes a BDC. The impact on U.S. exports to Vietnam is less certain.

Scholarly studies have also come to conflicting conclusions of the impact of the GSP program on international trade flows. Depending on the methodology used and the assumptions made, the studies have estimated the trade effect for GSP-eligible products as ranging from being negligible to increasing by over 60%.[39] For example, a 2006 study of EU trade preference programs estimated that the EU GSP program "does not significantly increase exports" for beneficiary countries.[40] Most of the studies calculated a less than 20% increase in GSP-eligible product exports.

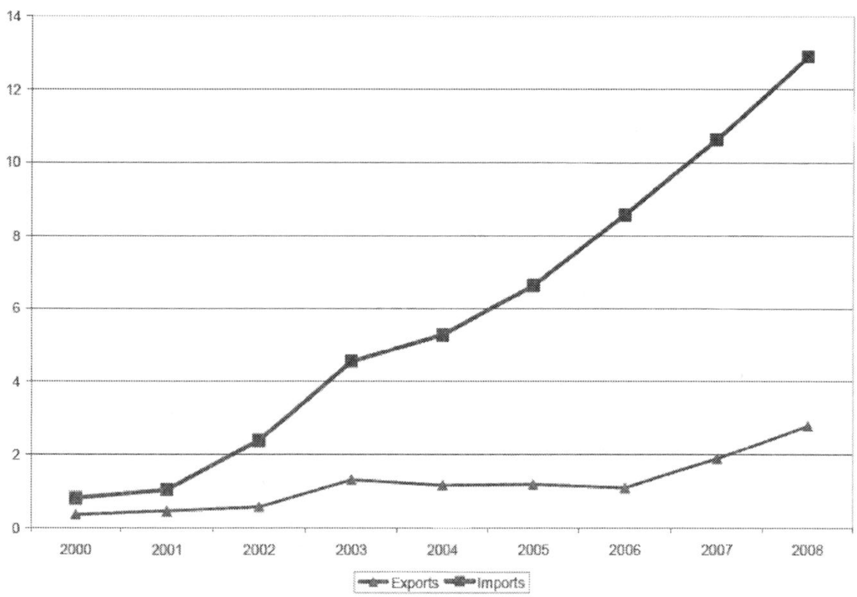

Figure 1. U.S. Merchandise Trade with Vietnam, 2000-2007, (U.S. $ Billions).

Although studies may differ on the trade effects of GSP programs, recent bilateral trade figures provide some evidence that the liberalization of U.S. trade relations with Vietnam does foster greater trade flows, particularly an increase in U.S. imports. Following the December 10, 2001 grant of NTR status to Vietnam, official U.S. trade statistics indicate that U.S. total merchandise trade with Vietnam doubled from $1.5 billion in 2001 to $3.0 billion in 2002 (See *Figure 1*). During that same time period, U.S. imports from Vietnam rose from $1.1 billion to $2.4 billion. By comparison, the increase in U.S. imports between 2000 and 2001 was just over $230 million. U.S. exports to Vietnam, by contrast, rose only slightly—increasing by less than $120 million—a comparable amount to the increase between 2000 and 2001. While acceptance into the U.S. GSP program is not as dramatic shift in trade status as NTR, the growth in post-NTR trade flows indicate that granting Vietnam BDC status under the Generalized System of Preferences should increase its exports to the United States.

Determining which Vietnamese exports will increase if the United States approves Vietnam's GSP application is also difficult. It would be logical to assume that most of Vietnam's export growth will occur among the GSP-eligible products. An examination of recent trade data, however, reveals that many of Vietnam's top exports are not GSP-eligible.

According to U.S. trade statistics, nearly 40% of U.S. imports from Vietnam in 2008 were articles of apparel (see *Table 1*). The next two top U.S. imports from Vietnam—furniture and footwear— together contributed another 20%. The fifth largest import from Vietnam in 2007 was crude oil. Taken together, the top five product categories accounted for over two-thirds of U.S. imports from Vietnam in 2007.

Table 1. Top Five U.S. Imports from Vietnam, 2008

Category	Value	Percentage of Total
Knitted or Crocheted Clothing (61)	$2,810,400,189	21.8%
Non-knitted or Crocheted Clothing (62)	$2,340,915,406	18.1%
Furniture (94)	$1,449,168,226	11.2%
Footwear (64)	$1,213,218,280	9.4%
Petroleum and Mineral Fuels (27)	$1,091,502,740	8.5%
Total Imports	$12,900,701,004	

Source: U.S. International Trade Commission. Numbers in parentheses refer to HTS chapter.

Vietnam's current top exports to the United States are unlikely to benefit from Vietnam's acceptance into the U.S. GSP program. Very few articles of apparel are GSP-eligible. Similarly, only a select group of furniture items are GSP-eligible—mostly light fixtures and mattresses. Footwear is also an import category that is largely excluded from the GSP program, as is crude oil. Therefore, Vietnam's top five exports to the United States are not likely to benefit from duty-free access under GSP.

Some of Vietnam's fastest growing exports to the United States, however, may benefit from duty-free access under GSP. Among Vietnam's top exports—product categories that provided more than 0.5% of U.S. imports from Vietnam—the growth leaders between 2000 and 2008 were: soaps (HTS[41] chapter 34), plastics and articles of plastic (39), paper and paper products (48), headgear (65), machinery (84), and electrical machinery (85). A comparison of these six product categories to the current list of GSP-eligible items reveals that three of these product categories— soaps, plastics and articles of plastic, machinery, and electrical machinery—are generally GSP-eligible, implying a greater likelihood of growth. Paper and paper products, as well as headgear, are not typically eligible for GSP benefits, so there is little chance of trade gains in these product categories.

The possibility of GSP eligibility may have the greatest implication for Vietnam's machinery and electrical machinery industries, since the Vietnamese government has been actively promoting its nation to overseas investors as a good location for machinery and electrical machinery operations. In addition, rising production costs in other parts of Asia—especially in China—are leading manufacturers to explore alternative locations for their Asian operations. Chinese companies, in particular, facing rising labor costs and the strengthening of the renminbi (RMB) against the U.S. dollar, may find the added bonus of GSP eligibility an incentive to relocate their final assembly operations to Vietnam. Such a shift could partially offset the general rise in the U.S. bilateral trade deficit with China, but would also increase the U.S. bilateral trade deficit with Vietnam. However, all of these trade effects would be limited in size by the competitive need limits (CNLs).

Vietnam's designation as a BDC under the GSP is likely to have little effect on U.S. producers of import-competing products, because domestic producers are largely shielded from severe economic impact under the preference due to the CNLs and other restrictions. Furthermore, if U.S. manufacturers of a product are adversely impacted by imports under GSP, they may petition that the product be removed from GSP eligibility.

U.S. exports to Vietnam may increase if Vietnam is designated as a BDC, but not as quickly as imports. Since the GSP is a non-reciprocal program, acceptance of Vietnam as a BDC will not provide similar duty-free treatment for U.S. exporters. In 2008, the United States exported about $2.8 billion in goods to Vietnam, up from approximately $368 million in 2000. Leading U.S. exports to Vietnam in 2008 included machinery, passenger motor vehicles, beef, cotton, polypropylene, scrap iron and steel, and lumber. However, many U.S. manufacturers use imports under GSP (such as wiring harnesses, brake and ignition parts, spectacle lenses, and insulated electrical conductors) as inputs for finished products that could later be exported to Vietnam and other GSP beneficiaries.

Issues for Congress

The GSP statute provides the President with the authority to designate any country a beneficiary developing country, provided the country complies with the conditions described in the statute. Therefore, Congress does not need to act to approve GSP status for Vietnam. The President is required to notify Congress of his intention, however.[42]

The Generalized System of Preferences program was set to expire on December 31, 2008, but was granted a one-year extension in sec. 4 of H.R. 7222 (passed House September 29, 2008, and October 3, 2008; passed Senate October 2, 2008). The legislation was signed into law on October 16, 2008 (P.L. 110-436).

Congress could also authorize or instruct the President to designate—or *not* to designate— Vietnam as a BDC, either as part of the legislation to extend the GSP program or in separate legislation. For example, S. 3678 (110th Congress), the Vietnam Human Rights Act of 2008, would prohibit the grant of GSP status unless the President certifies that Vietnam has met certain human rights conditions. In addition, Congress could pass legislation stipulating additional criteria for the President to consider when deciding to confer BDC status to Vietnam. Such legislation could also include specific restrictions on GSP-eligible products for Vietnam and/or the size of CNLs.

Over the past decade, Congress has debated a number of issues with respect to U.S.-Vietnam relations, particularly Vietnam's growing and increasingly liberalized economy and its human rights record. The United States also has a sizeable and growing foreign assistance program in Vietnam, and the two countries are expanding their strategic relations. All these issues may factor into the debate over GSP membership.

End Notes

[1] 73 F.R. 35173, June 20, 2008.
[2] White House, Office of the President, "Joint Statement Between the United States of America and the Socialist Republic of Vietnam," Press Release, June 25, 2008.
[3] The text of the U.S.-Vietnam TIFA is available on the USTR's web page at http://www.ustr.gov/assets/ Trade_Agreements/TIFA/asset_upload_file81_12935.pdf.
[4] 19 U.S.C. §§ 2461-2467, as amended.
[5] 19 U.S.C. § 2462; section 502 of P.L. 93-618, as amended. For a more detailed discussion of the GSP program, see CRS Report RL33663, *Generalized System of Preferences: Background and Renewal Debate*, by Vivian C. Jones.
[6] These countries are Australia, Canada, European Union member states, Iceland, Japan, Monaco, New Zealand, Norway, and Switzerland.
[7] 19 U.S.C. § 2462, as amended.
[8] Ibid.
[9] 19 U.S.C. § 2463(a)(1).
[10] 19 U.S.C. § 2463(b).
[11] 19 U.S.C. § 2463(c).
[12] 19 U.S.C. § 2463(a)(2).
[13] 73 F.R. 35173, June 20, 2008.
[14] Public comments concerning Vietnam's GSP eligibility are posted on the USTR website: http://www.ustr.gov/assets/Trade_Development/Preference_Programs/GSP/ GSP_Review_to_Consider_Designation_of_Socialist_Republic_of_Vietnam_as_a_Beneficiary_Developing_Country_ Under_the_GSP/asset_upload_file576_15064.pdf.
[15] The TPSC was established by Section 242 of the Trade Expansion Act of 1962 (19 U.S.C. § 1872) and implemented by Executive Order 12188, as amended. The President delegated the administration of the GSP program to the committee in sec. 8 of Executive Order 11846, as amended.
[16] 19 C.F.R. § 2007.2(e).
[17] For more information, see CRS Report RL33316, *U.S.-Vietnam Relations in 2008: Background and Issues for Congress*, by Mark E. Manyin.
[18] For more information about pre-Doi Moi working conditions in Vietnam, see CRS Report RL30896, *Vietnam's Labor Rights Regime: An Assessment*, by Mark E. Manyin et al.
[19] Government of the Socialist Republic of Vietnam. "Statement re Supporting Documentation [of GSP Status]," May 9, 2008, p. 9.
[20] "Vietnam: Internet Writer Tran Quoc Hien Sentenced," *English Pen*, May 25, 2007.
[21] Testimony by Sophie Richardson, Asia Advocacy Director, Human Rights Watch, before the House Committee on Foreign Affairs Subcommittee on International Organizations, Human Rights, and Oversight, November 6, 2007.
[22] Government of the Socialist Republic of Vietnam. "Statement re Supporting Documentation [of GSP Status]," May 9, 2008, p. 10.
[23] Ibid.
[24] "Government Units to Tackle Labour Disputes," *Vietnam Net*, February 21, 2009.

[25] "Solutions to Labourers' Strikes Require Efforts from All Sides," *Vietnam Net*, September 5, 2008.

[26] Author's interview with unnamed industrial sources.

[27] CRS Report RL33490, *Vietnam PNTR Status and WTO Accession: Issues and Implications for the United States*, by Mark E. Manyin, William H. Cooper, and Bernard A. Gelb.

[28] Ibid.

[29] Ibid.

[30] Comments by AFL-CIO and other organizations on Vietnam's GSP Application, submitted to USTR on August 4, 2008; available online at http://www.ustr.gov/assets/Trade_ Development/Preference_Programs/GSP/ GSP_Review_to_Consider_Designation_of_Socialist_Republic_of_Vietnam_as_a_Beneficiary_Developing_Country_ Under_the_GSP/asset_upload_file576_15064.pdf.

[31] Ibid.

[32] Ibid.

[33] "Trade dress" refers to the physical appearance—color, shape, textile, graphics, and/or size—of a product.

[34] Quote from the organization's home page—http://www.protectvietworkers.com/.

[35] "Vietnam: New Round of Arrests Target Democracy Activists," *Human Rights Watch*, September 12, 2008.

[36] Nga Pham, "Prayers and Protests in Vietnam," BBC News, September 2, 2008.

[37] "Funeral Services Held for Dissident Patriarch of Banned Vietnamese Buddhist Church," *Associated Press*, July 11, 2008.

[38] For an explanation of the technical problems of conducting such a projection, see Craig R. MacPhee and Victor Iwuagwu Oguledo, "The Trade Effects of the U.S. Generalized System of Preference," *Atlantic Economic Journal*, December 1991, Vol. 19, No. 4, pp. 19-26.

[39] MacPhee and Oguledo, op. cit.

[40] Maria Persson and Fredrik Wilhelmsson, "Assessing the Effects of EU Trade Preferences for Developing Countries," Working Papers, Lund University, Department of Economics, 2006:4.

[41] Harmonized Tariff Schedule.

[42] Under the provisions of 19 U.S.C. 2462(f)(1), the President must notify Congress 60 days prior to the designation of a least-developed BDC; no time period is specified for BDC designation.

INDEX

A

B

C

D

J

K

L

M

N

O

P

Q

R

S

T

U

V

W

Y

Z